AGING STRONG

AGING STRONG

The Extraordinary Gift of a Longer Life

Bud Harris, Ph.D.

Daphne Publications

DAPHNE PUBLICATIONS, AN IMPRINT OF SPES, INC.

Harris, Clifton T. Bud
Aging strong: the extraordinary gift of a longer life
Bud Harris
ISBN Nonfiction
ISBN: 0692726748
ISBN 13: 9780692726747
Library of Congress Control Number: 2016908974
Spes, Inc, Asheville, NC

1. Aging 2. Psychology 3. Jungian psychology 4. Spirituality

Also by Bud Harris, PhD:

Becoming Whole: A Jungian Guide to Individuation

Radical Hope and the Healing Power of Illness: A Jungian Guide to Exploring the Body, Mind, Spirit Connection to Healing

The Search for Self and the Search for God

Cracking Open: A Memoir of Struggling, Passages, and Transformations

Sacred Selfishness: A Guide to Living a Life of Substance

The Father Quest: Rediscovering an Elemental Force

Resurrecting the Unicorn: Masculinity in the 21st Century

The Fire and the Rose: The Wedding of Spirituality and Sexuality

Knowing the Questions Living the Answers: A Jungian Guide Through the Paradoxes of Peace, Conflict and Love that Mark a Lifetime

Coauthored with Massimilla Harris, PhD:

Into the Heart of the Feminine: Facing the Death Mother Archetype to Reclaim Love, Strength, and Vitality

Like Gold Through Fire: Understanding the Transforming Power of Suffering

The Art of Love: The Craft of Relationship: A Practical Guide for Creating the Loving Relationships We Want

CONTENTS

To all of you who want to enter the most important years of your lives as seekers of a new way that deepens our spirits and blossoms into the fullness of life's potentials and the richness these efforts can bring into the world.

*Life behaves as if it were going on, and so I
think it is better for an old person to live on,
to look forward to the next day, as if he had to
spend centuries, and then he lives properly. But
when he is afraid, when he doesn't look forward, he looks back, he petrifies, he gets stiff,
and he dies before his time.
But when he's living and looking forward to
the great adventure that is ahead, then he
lives, and that is about what the unconscious is
intending to do...Man cannot stand a meaningless life.*

C. G. Jung

Acknowledgments

*T*his book is a product of my years of experiences and reflections. A special thank-you is due to the men, women, and
children whom I've been privileged to know and work with
in my professional life. I want to assure all of them, who have
labored to understand themselves and to grow through life's
challenges, that the stories in this book are fictionalized com-
positions. They have evolved from my thirty-five-plus years of
experience and are typical of real-life situations without being
based on the actual experiences of any particular person.

    I have a special debt of gratitude to the Jungian analysts,
mentors, and teachers I encountered during my training at
the C. G. Jung Institute in Zurich, Switzerland, who were in
their seventh and eighth decades. Their presence opened many
doors for me and helped initiate me into an amazing life.

Preface

This book has been written for you if you are one of us who wants to grow old. If you are one of us who wants to thrive psychologically and find spiritual well-being, wisdom, and wonder as our bodies slow down. One who wants to be able to say, "I have been given much, and I have given something in return." This book is written for you if you are willing to recognize that we live in a new period of history. Today we can live longer and with more vitality than people ever have. Our reality means we can choose to seize this opportunity for living the fourth quarter of our lives creatively, lovingly, and joyfully.

For more than thirty-five years, I have practiced as a psychologist and Zurich-trained Jungian analyst. I have lectured, given workshops around the country, and corresponded with readers of my books for more than twenty-five years. In every audience, people who are in or approaching the fourth quarter of their lives have been the most intensely interested in living lives of meaning, of authenticity, and as expressions of their true selves.

I never thought I would be as old as I am now, and I am even more surprised at how excited I am about my life and work. That's right—my work. As I am on the cusp of my eighth decade, I find that I am living with more clarity, passion, and purpose than I ever have, even though I have always considered myself a purpose-driven person. I have spent some time wondering how this happened and why I didn't see it coming. At the same time, I've found myself wondering why I spent so many years listening to those so-called "practical" voices and worrying about my retirement fund and all of the dangers and disasters that could befall me as I was approaching this stage in my life.

A substantial part of the answers to these questions is that I live in a new era—an era in which practical or conventional wisdom does not fit, an era of great opportunity for so many of us in our society. Practical or conventional wisdom is always based on the past, and the past is not repeating itself for those of us in or entering the fourth quarter of life today. At my age, my father's father was long dead. Suddenly, we are in a time when we can have as many or more productive years after age sixty than we had before what is commonly thought of as midlife. This reality means we need to reimagine our entire approach to how we are going to live and meet the opportunities in the fourth quarter of our lives.

■ ■ ■

For decades, in the Jungian circles that I am a part of and in much of our society, the midlife crisis has been looked at as a signal to turn inward, to learn to know ourselves better, to become more spiritually oriented, and to spend more time in the search for inner wholeness. Midlife is such a turning point.

But as I look back at it thirty-five years later, I realize that it was more than a turning point. It was a time when I began awakening to the fact that my life wasn't what I thought it was. I discovered I was living in the mythological "wasteland," the land of living an inauthentic life defined by cultural norms and others' expectations. As I awakened, it seemed as if my life was a play whose script had been written by society, family, church, and traditions. My character had been shaped and driven by the struggles in my family and my culture and, as a result, the struggles within myself. As a group, we call this particular awakening, this turning point, a midlife crisis. It has almost become a cliché to say a crisis and an opportunity are two sides of the same coin, but it is true. Our midlife crises are opportunities to choose new roads for our lives. By new roads, I don't mean just a new job or a new partner, but a chance to change the entire design that shapes who we are, our values, our purpose, and our capacities to feel contentment, love, and joy.

I have discovered that when we are entering the fourth quarter of our lives, generally after the age of sixty, we face another turning point, another crisis that is just as powerful as the one we faced at midlife, we also find ourselves in a new wasteland. Exploring our need for a new awakening and a new vision to live by, as we face and enter the fourth quarter of our lives, and how we can do this is the major focus of this book.

To move from awakening to living a new life with new opportunities involves facing, remembering, and developing new perspectives on our life's history. Approaching this task is like sinking a mineshaft deep into the earth of our own being in order to bring out the gold ore of our best selves and potentials. Then we have to refine the ore even further than we have in the past in order to make it a priceless part of ourselves.

We have been conditioned into a society in which the cold eyes of science, practicality, and the "bottom-line" mentality have built a culture that lives in denial of its pain and struggles and the suffering that has the potential to teach us compassion and wisdom. None of us are really free from the many kinds of pain in life, and only a few of us have learned how to glean wisdom and spiritual depth from our pain. Almost all of us have become experts at anesthetizing ourselves and, for example, are addicted to something, whether it is food, TV, electronic gadgets, alcohol, drugs, medications, golf, shopping, or other things, including busyness.

Those of us in the fourth quarter of life have the greatest opportunity to slow down and examine how the world we are living in is affecting us, robbing us of time and nourishment. We need and have the capacity to choose a life of community and relationships, a life lived for a higher purpose and in defiance of the alienation supported by the structure of everyday existence in our society. Recent medical and brain research shows that our relationships with ourselves and with others are keystones in a life that is healthy, joyful, and long lasting. Yet, paradoxically, our society's structures have become our worst enemy in our efforts to live this way.

The heart of Jungian psychology, which is the position that I am writing from, tells us that our challenges, dysfunctions, and diseases are the symptoms of a life that is being blocked from fulfilling its true purpose and the love and confidence it is capable of enjoying. These symptoms are the efforts of our greater Self to heal our past and open us to a more fulfilling version of life. This greater Self—the Self in Jungian terms—is the true center of who we are, and it reflects the image of the Divine within us. It contains the inherent pattern of our true potentials, our life forces, and its purpose is to bring us into the full expression and experience of our lives.

This perspective is very different from the typical approach we take toward ourselves in terms of trying to fix or solve our difficulties or even to attempt to heal our emotional wounds in order to get ourselves back on track or back to "normal."

■ ■ ■

As we encounter our midlife or our fourth-quarter turning points, we may find ourselves confused. This confusion is caused when we experience symptoms of fear, lethargy, depression, anxiety, and physical ailments. In these cases, our symptoms are the signs that we are facing a major passage and a transformation period in our lives that we have little awareness of and even less knowledge of how to approach. We have no map for these journeys and no set of cultural rituals or initiation rites to guide us through these passages. The simple reality is that, in the past, most people didn't live in good health long enough to face a fourth-quarter challenge. This is a new challenge for us.

So in this book, I want to share a map that is based on the essential pattern of the hero's or heroine's journey in mythology as a symbol of the journey of transforming our personalities. I will also share my own personal experience of this process and my professional experience, for more than twenty years, of working with men and women struggling to make this passage.

In the balance of this book, we will explore how to:

Recognize and begin the called-for process of transforming ourselves and enlarging our lives.

Decrease our everyday and long-standing fears.

Expand our understanding of love and how it shapes our lives from birth until death.

Reimagine how to deal with the places we feel stuck or trapped or have lost sight of new possibilities.

Reenvision our failures, their true meaning, and the possibilities they contain.

Restore and renew our vision of joy and living with enthusiasm as being more important than the search for happiness and the avoidance of pain.

■ ■ ■

Like all serious books of this nature, this book represents a journey. It is a journey out of the wasteland of an old way of life that is ending and into a new awakening, as we face the fourth quarter of our lives. Chapter 1, "A Time for Being All in the Game," will give you a vision of the new reality we are living in, along with its challenges, opportunities, and potentials. Chapter 2, "Becoming Fully Engaged," is an invitation to see how we can open ourselves to a new version of life, one that is a bigger, more intense, more alive version, with new opportunities. Chapter 3, "Facing Dangerous Moments," discusses some of the pitfalls we face, the danger of falling back into the illusionary safety of a life defined by fear, and other norms of our marketing-driven culture and what we think other people expect.

In chapter 4, "Bringing Our Lives Together," we will examine the importance of looking at the story of our lives and getting a better sense of the context of who we are; how we are living; and how to understand, change, and transform the stories we have been caught in.

In chapter 5, "Harnessing the Strength of Our Needs and Desires," we will search intensely the ways we have been limited by how our personalities were formed, including our attitudes, our values, and our fears. My purpose in this chapter is to help you find the knowledge that can free you from fear and put you in touch with potentials that have lain dormant in you for years, waiting to be discovered and lived. Chapter 6, "Reflections on the Journey—Singed, Scorched, and Seasoned," will help you get a new vision of the meaning of consciousness and creativity. You will see the results of the inner journey reflected in life and values and the new strength, clarity, and vitality it brings. In chapter 7, some of "The Spiritual Challenges of Aging," will emerge. I will share some of my own perspectives for confronting death, what that means for us, and what that means for how we can live our best lives. Living our best lives can also teach us how we are "dying into life" all the time. I share how, in my personal and professional experiences, I have learned that a life fully lived requires that we are individually aware of how we are living, have a vital connection with our inner lives, and are participating consciously in their development. I am convinced that when we live this way, our lives will find their completion in a state of peace and joy.

■ ■ ■

By the time we are approaching the fourth quarter in our lives, we have experienced our share of adversities, trials, failures, perhaps illnesses, and successes, as well as setbacks and heartaches. As we transition into the fourth quarter in our lives, just like our passage at midlife, it isn't enough to just say that today is a new day. All that we have experienced has formed the neural pathways and connections in our brains. This is particularly true in our "feeling" brain, and we need to engage in the kinds of experiences that will restructure our emotional brains through building new neural networks.

In other words, we must become engaged in a process of radical self-exploration and of knowing the realities of our emotional pasts as thoroughly as possible. It is to our distinct advantage to commit ourselves to change and to begin the process of expanding into a larger, more authentic life. We also need to be engaged with other people to facilitate this transformation within ourselves. Bringing depth, understanding, and compassion into the experiences of our pasts becomes the doorway to whom we may become and the source of the courage that can open that door.

I have asked myself more than once, "Is it worth all this effort?" Then I have to ask myself these questions: "Is living with love and courage worth the effort? Is living from a stable center worth the effort? Is refusing to hide behind appearances, in isolation and loneliness, even in sorrow and bitterness worth the effort?" These questions bring me back to my original question: "Is it worth all of this effort?" The answer for me must be "Yes!" Whatever the effort for a life lived passionately, for a life that is loved and is loving is worth what it takes to gain it. I am convinced that living this way is the highest goal I can attain and that to love life is to love the Divine.

■ ■ ■

As one of the mature members of our society, I also have to ask myself whether I really have any other ethical alternative to this challenge. I no longer believe that hope can be in the younger generation. They are struggling today. They are having trouble finding a place in the world. We are seeing this in our practice as we never have before. People in their twenties and early thirties are having a lot of difficulty finding traction in their identities and direction in their lives. Those who do, and they are many, are burdened with economic struggles and the challenges of raising families in a hard-minded world. Our age group is where the hope and responsibility for change lies. We need to use the foundation of our accomplishments and the potential of the compassion and wisdom we can develop to bring hope back into the world.

If, as the mature members of our culture, we look around us, we see that the miracle of life is not being lived very well. Some kind of violence haunts and threatens our daily lives. Statistics tell us that depression, anxiety, and addictions cost our country billions of dollars a year, and these costs only hint at the mountains of suffering behind them. These costs and the extent of the suffering are growing quickly and are reaching down into the lives of our children and grandchildren at an alarming rate. Heart disease has become a metaphor for our drive and our loneliness. Other illnesses and how long we may live personally are clearly related to the amount of fear, stress, love, and affection we have or don't have in our lives. And most of all, we need to remember that transformation, love, vision, and purpose begin within ourselves, are tempered and forged in our relationships, and then spread out to the people around us.

We, the people our age, are the key to changing everything for the better. The first step is seeking a bigger version of ourselves. Our modern brain research teaches us that real change within ourselves doesn't take a little time—it takes a lot of time. But it also keeps our brains active and vital. I'll share more about how to give this gift to ourselves and to life later in the book. For now, let me point out how this book is designed to help you apply the knowledge in it and choose the road to *aging strong*.

First, you can read the book straight through, and then choose what you would like to apply from it in your life. This approach, which often includes underlining key passages and making notes in the margins or in your journal, can help you become emotionally and mentally connected to the flow of ideas and suggestions in the book and how you can use them. I also urge you to take an additional step and get one or more friends to join you by reading and discussing the book.

The journey into a bigger vision of life as we age and the realization of the opportunity we have together are better when they are shared with a friend or a small reading group, in which you can discuss what you have read and exchange experiences and ideas with one another. This approach will help you grow stronger and more centered in yourself, psychologically and spiritually. Real growth is never an isolated experience and, as our brain research reminds us, is enhanced by having a small community of like-minded friends.

■ ■ ■

The fourth quarter of life is a special time to heal the past and deepen our humanity in the present. It is time to grow, to flourish creatively, and to fashion a better world. It is a time of great opportunity spiritually, psychologically, and collectively—a time for love to bear its fruit. Because I know the benefits of this journey, I invite you to join it. I hope that you will find this book a friend and companion as you begin a new journey.

1

A Time for Being All in the Game

As I entered the fourth quarter of my life, I thought I would be entering a final phase. Instead, I discovered I was experiencing a new beginning. Mythologies, the stories of our eternal journeys, show new beginnings as our initiations into new phases of our lives and symbolically outline the structure of the transitional journey we must go through, emotionally and psychologically. This new phase brings a new approach to life and is further symbolized by the mythological hero or heroine's journey; new dreams and values must be won and the confrontation with ourselves and life bring us new strength, clarity, humility, and a new appreciation of the offerings of our hearts.

Dr. Jung was clear when he said that, in the larger picture, nature doesn't make mistakes, and if we are now living longer, there is a larger purpose that we are meant to fulfill. In order to face this new opportunity, or as I see it, this new destiny for us, we have to take a second look at our natural urge for the safety, stability, and protection that we seek in economic security. This doesn't mean we should live carelessly. It means that we should keep in mind that we are always called to live beyond society's fears and norms if we want to fulfill our lives. We will always have to face conflicts between our calls for adventure and our desires for comfort and our security.

To begin with, we must acknowledge that we are facing a period in human life that is new, and that it has meaning as well as challenges. Properly understanding this new phase and translating it into a new way of life is crucial for us. If we don't understand it, the moment of transition can pass, leaving us sinking into or stuck in the vestiges of our old life and the limitations of social norms. In many ways, we may feel like we are living in threatening times. But for people my age, I think we are living in challenging and exciting times. Our old models for aging are becoming boring and meaningless. We can explore new ways of living, understanding ourselves, and growing that may result in opportunities that are more unique, personal, fulfilling, and loving than ever before. The choice is up to us and depends on whether we're willing to take our journeys into inner knowledge seriously enough to balance the power of the influences of the images— images of fear and the good life—that our marketing culture is imposing on us.

Dr. Jung is correct when he says that living longer has a purpose. The imperative of life is to grow. We can grow psychologically and spiritually for as long as we are alive. Growing in these areas is a purpose that supports our lives. It is a purpose in itself. But it also brings *new purposes* into our lives. For this growth to take place, we need to ally ourselves with life, love, and the courage it takes to face the challenges that growth entails. Easier to say than to do, you might think. But if we keep life's basic purpose in mind, alive in our reflections, these allegiances may take root within us sooner than we expect. And if, instead, we fail to grow, we will stagnate and begin to deteriorate, no matter how good we are at presenting the public faces we are hiding behind.

When Dr. Jung said we must be able to look forward in old age to the next day and to look forward to the great adventure that is ahead, he was making life's "imperative to grow" personal. As long as we are alive, we must be able to dream of the future, of a better world or better ways of life. We are also invited by our greater Self to dream new dreams of creativity and fresh ways of expressing ourselves, as many great artists have into their nineties.

Our self-knowledge is meant to grow and develop throughout our lives as well. It grows best with our help, our attentiveness, and our reflections and by interacting with our unconscious, as I will explain in the next few chapters. But our self-knowledge also grows out of sight at times, until it bursts into our awareness through a building up of tensions that ultimately are seeking to break through our former limits.

My experience of cancer was one of those informative breakthroughs that redirected my life, my goals, and my frame of mind. I've seen many other examples of these breakthroughs taking place. I remember reading about John on a popular news website. John had retired from the post office at age sixty-five, and he spent the next two years in a moderately severe depression. As he worked his way out of his depression, he took a job in the garden department of a big box home remodeling and repair store. At the time of his interview, he was in his midnineties. He told the interviewer he had found his vocation, and it was to help people bring beauty into their lives and homes.

I also remember Elizabeth. Elizabeth had been a primary school teacher who retired at age sixty. She spent the next few years in Jungian analysis, trying to figure out how to redirect her life onto a path that was more fulfilling than her previous career had been. As a result of her inner explorations, she went back to school, got her doctorate in ministry, and became a pastoral counselor. When I knew her, she was seventy-two years old and studying at the C. G. Jung Institute in Zurich, Switzerland.

I also recall a man I met in a men's group I had been asked to start in the early 1990s. Robert had been a general surgeon. He said he had retired because the changes in his profession were happening faster than he could, or cared to, keep up with. But now, at age seventy-five, he was spending every other month in a hospital in Africa where he said his knowledge and skills were still far ahead of the game. Cynthia was another person who came to mind as I was writing this chapter. At seventy-four, she had just finished learning Spanish and had joined the Peace Corps.

Living passionately means facing our fears and the troubles we are encountering, in order to eventually achieve a state of inner harmony. If we are unable to live passionately, we'll have the tendency to repress our strong emotions and either project our inner conflicts outside of ourselves or absorb them inside of ourselves as depression, lethargy, bitterness, or some illness. These conflicts represent a desire for life that has been blocked by some other force within us, such as fear, conventional wisdom, or the rigid and limiting stances of parents whose images are still very alive in our psyches.

It takes courage to dream, to face our futures and the limiting forces within us. It takes courage to be determined that, as we slow down physically, we are going to grow even more psychologically and spiritually. Courage, the philosopher Aristotle taught us, is the most important of all the virtues, because without it we can't practice any of the others. Courage is the nearest star that can guide our growth. Maya

Angelou said we must be courageous about facing and exploring our personal histories. We must find the courage to care and to create internally, as well as externally, and as she said, we need the courage "to create ourselves daily as Christians, as Jews, as Muslims, as thinking, caring, laughing, loving human beings."

Like myself, Elizabeth, John, Robert, and Cynthia found that making the transition into the fourth quarter of life was an initiation into a new vision of themselves and how they saw their lives, if they were going to continue to live authentically and vitally. They, too, found themselves living with more passion and purpose in the fourth quarter of their lives than they had before. Initiation as a process of transition requires that we accept the reality of the change we need to make. Often, acceptance begins in a state of confusion and maybe even depression, as we must stop and examine more fully who we are. If we can then begin the hero or heroine's journey into ourselves, we will find inner support to help us through the conflicting feelings and elements within us. The journey that we will make in the balance of this book will help us reconcile our inner conflicts, strike a balance within ourselves, and will be followed by a true sense of liberation.

Choosing Life

In his story of the hero's journey and its meaning, *The Hero with a Thousand Faces*, the mythologist Joseph Campbell explains that when you follow someone else's path, you always go astray. The hero or heroine has to set off by himself or herself, to leave an old world and its old ways behind. When we begin this journey, symbolized in the myth, we must venture into the unknown life before us without a map and where there is no clear route. We must confront our own monster, not someone else's; explore our own inner labyrinth; and endure our own ordeal before we can find what is missing in our lives. Then, having become transformed, we can bring something of value back to ourselves and the world we have left behind. In the words of *The Quest of the Holy Grail*, each knight must enter the forest where it is darkest and there is no path. The wasteland in the *Grail* legend is the place where people live inauthentic lives, blindly following the norms and conventional wisdom of society and doing what other people expect them to. Choosing life is choosing to enter the forest where no one else has. It is choosing to accept the reality of the transition in front of you, to let go of your old life and old self and be initiated into the new period of your life as a new person. This choice means to choose life in its fullest sense and undergo our journey of transformation as I did and as Elizabeth, John, Robert, and Cynthia did. There is one simple reason for making this choice. *It is life enhancing.*

When we choose to enter the forest alone, we are making a radical choice to confront our lives and feelings as we look for a new vocation and destiny in the fourth quarter of our lives. Both Joseph Campbell and Dr. Jung assure us that if we pursue this work religiously, helping hands and a sacred influence will evolve from this work into our lives. Dr. Jung goes on to remind us that we have an inner guide that can lead us, an inner friend that can support us and an inner aspect of the Divine that will help bring new vitality, vision, and resilience into our lives. But these inner resources don't just drop into our laps. We must choose to seek them, to be open to them, and to welcome them.

Dr. Jung describes this inner friend and guide as the Self. Jungians capitalize the word "Self" in order to separate it from what we think of as our everyday self, or in psychological terms, our ego. I like to refer to these two aspects of ourselves as our little self and our big Self. But this big Self is much more than a friend and guide. It also stands for the archetypal image of our fullest potentials and the promising unity within our personality as a whole. We think of it as the unifying principle in our personality and therefore it represents the central position of authority in relationship to our psychological life and personal destiny. In addition to containing the patterns of our potentials and the life we are meant to fulfill in our unique way, the big Self also contains the creative life force that seeks to compel our growth. This life force will attempt to lure us or push us toward wholeness, meaning toward the completion of our patterns of potentials. And incidentally, our life force doesn't retire—ever. As we age it simply switches its emphasis to the parts of us like our spirit and psychology that can continue to grow. In other words, as our bodies slow down, our spirit and personality can blossom. If we are on the wrong track with our life or are caught in the shell of a rigidified life, the Self will seek to crack this shell, and it may use anxiety, depression, dysfunctional behaviors, and even an illness to accomplish this cracking open.

In this case, our problems are not our enemies. They are the alarm system going off through our spirit, mind, and body connections telling us that we are living in a self-alienating manner, oblivious to or even against the patterns of our potentials and our life forces. In these situations, we must learn to try to listen to our big Self, as it is trying to communicate with us through our emotions, life events, dreams, and symptoms. If we don't learn how to listen to our inner alarm system, it will repeat itself more and more seriously until it is heard or it is too late. I will share a map and methods for this kind of listening in the rest of this book.

Because of this inherent power in the big Self, which is so integral to our lives, I consider it as being within our DNA, and it behaves that way in our lives. Because it is demanding to be recognized within each of us in the Western tradition, we often refer to it as the "image of the Divine" within us. For me, it has been the source of what I consider my experiences of the Divine. Many of the great religions have the goal of bringing unity to the personality and consciousness from the psychological perspective.

The reality is that if we are going to realize our full growth and live our unique lives, if we are going to create an inner environment that supports our growth vitality and love, if we are going to achieve a true sense of peace and strength, then at some point in our lives, we have to become aware of this other center within us—the big Self. The big Self contains a greater intelligence and vitality than our ego (our little self or everyday personality).

Dr. Jung was fond of saying, "If we do not carefully heed life's hints, then life will hit us in the face." In other words, vitality and growth do not come from just taking life's hints. We also need to search for their meaning and their source. This search is making the conscientious inner journey that is necessary to help us discover the blueprint of our potentials. The next step is to consciously assist in moving the contents in our unconscious, as they are presented by the big Self, one by one, into our conscious personality, in order to refine them and live them. In our mature years, this process is the true source of our growth and vitality.

■ ■ ■

The availability of this inner wealth at many times and in different circumstances in our lives means that choice isn't a simple one-time deal. It means that choice is an evolving journey that must be made at every turning point in our lives. We have to choose to become a seeker again in each case. As I have practiced, seeing men and women in their sixties, seventies, and eighties over the last twenty years, I've seen that making this choice at any age can bring a revitalized life and a new vision of one's future.

Entering and being in the fourth quarter of life may be one of the best times in our life to open the door of our cage of traditional thinking and step outside of it, where we find opportunity and hope.

Let me repeat this statement as strongly as I can: we must choose to be seekers of new and deeper self-knowledge and self-awareness, rather than allowing ourselves to become passive in the face of life and slipping into hollow versions of our potential selves.

This choice cannot work without practice. Like any spiritual path or physical training program, we must practice our reflections regularly, even when it makes us sore or seems discouraging. The reality is that the more we practice, the more depth and strength we gain. The more power we give to the process and the more we invest in it, the larger the return is for us.

This work isn't easy, but very little worth having or worth earning comes easily. To choose life means choosing a commitment to the journey and devotion to it. It means to be dedicated; it means to go deep enough within ourselves to touch the life force within us, to love it, to listen to it, and to let it love us. In dialoging and listening to my cancer, it told me how I was blocking my life force and creativity. You may be sure that this was a scary and difficult process for me. It was even more difficult to get my head around the idea that an illness that was so frightening to me could be telling me how I needed to transform myself and redirect my life. John, whom I mentioned earlier, had to discover his new life by working through his depression and so did Elizabeth after she retired. I carefully explain how to approach our unconscious in this most rewarding way in my book *Sacred Selfishness*.

On the other hand, when we learn to act as if we are running out of energy or see ourselves as old, impaired, or damaged, we tend to give our authority over to others and/or decide to defensively disassociate from our potentials. All too often, society and the people around us will support our making a decision to take a positive attitude that can cause us to be more pleasing to them while we are actually spending the rest of our lives as shadow versions of our former selves.

Becoming a seeker is a choice that we are often forced to make in the halls of confusion or fear and when we are facing a crisis. But in the long run, nothing is more destructive than self-alienation, feeling powerless, hopeless, and unloved by myself and the Divine.

So let me invite you to become a seeker, to choose life, and to remember..."Whatever you can do, or dream you can, begin it. Boldness has genius, power, and magic in it."

2

Becoming Fully Engaged

What can open us to the call to a new future? What changed in John, Elizabeth, Robert, and Cynthia that put them on paths that they had never considered before? I also had to ask myself, what changed in me that revitalized my vocation and redirected it? Certainly these paths and potentials must have been dormant somewhere inside us. The question is not so much why we weren't aware of these potentials and the desires behind them. The real question is, "How did we discover them and bring to life?"

Most of the people I know and have worked with have made this transition and moved either into a renewed sense of vocation or into a new vocation. Please notice I am using the word *vocation* here and not *job* or *career*. A vocation is something that is a calling and has purpose and meaning, no matter what kind of work it is. John's job was simply being a salesperson in a big box store. But his purpose was to help bring beauty into people's lives

and homes. By having such a purpose in his life, he could be glad to get up in the morning, happy in his work, and on the majority of his days, he could come home with a feeling of satisfaction and gratitude for what he was able to accomplish. Having a vocation also made his interactions with people during the day, for the most part, joyful and invigorating.

But moving in these directions isn't easy. All of the people I worked with, including myself, had gone through periods—and sometimes extended periods—of confusion, anxiety, depression, and even illness, coupled with some dedicated work in psychotherapy or Jungian analysis. Life had actually pushed John, Elizabeth, Robert, and me into periods that called for reflection and for us to turn our focus inward.

Life and human nature calls us to stop and do this kind of reflection whenever we are facing a transitional period of letting our old personality structures go and developing fresh ways of looking at the importance of our lives and of becoming open to something greater within ourselves. I have referred to this "something" as the big Self, our greater Self that contains our potential for new purpose, meaning, and vitality in our future. By becoming receptive to this greater Self within us, we simultaneously increase our capacities to thrive, to grow in our love of life and in wisdom, and to give back some of our best potentials to the world.

At this stage in our lives, we don't choose our calling; we have become mature enough to realize that our "calling" chooses us. In other words, neither our ego nor our small self chooses our calling; it is our capacity to listen to our big Self that actually lets us "be called." By focusing inward and accepting the necessity for our old personality to go through a period of transition and transformation, we become receptive to our greater Self and the dynamic new potentials it contains. During this process, in which we begin to breathe deeply and listen with our whole selves, we become open to possibilities way beyond what our small selves could have previously imagined. As this process continues and we learn to trust our own hearts and this deeper wisdom, either our calling or callings will evolve into our awareness from within ourselves, or we will recognize it when it comes to us in our outer lives. It is important to remember our calling or callings can cover a wide range of expressions and activities. They are not restricted to what we normally think of as jobs or professions.

As mentioned, it is always helpful for me to remember there is a purpose to my life, and there are potentials to be fulfilled, even if at times they seem hidden to me. Some of my biggest turning points and heartbreaks have only made sense when I was looking back and reflecting on them. When I was experiencing them, I was often too saturated in the disappointment, confusion, or pain to realize that my big Self will be seeking to guide my life even through these times and events.

We need to overcome our collective indoctrination into the idea that we are always supposed to be happy, have a positive attitude, and do everything for ourselves and by ourselves. According to the well-known author Barbara Ehrenreich in her important book, *Bright-sided: How the Relentless Promotion of Positive Thinking Is Undermining America*, we must face up to the reality that we live under "the tyranny of positive thinking" in our culture. This illusion causes us to blame ourselves for everything from simple unhappiness to cancer—without examining our reality at all. The idea that we are always supposed to be happy, think positively, and handle everything ourselves without bothering anyone else or missing a few minutes of being productive encourage us to deny reality, appear to submit cheerfully to our misfortunes, and blame ourselves too quickly for our difficult circumstances.

It might be easier for us if we could say that when we face a major transition point, like moving into the fourth quarter of life, that our glass of meaning and purpose isn't to be seen half-full because it is lying shattered on the floor. Then the question for us becomes, "Are we going to play like we still have a glass half-full or are we going to face reality, clean up the pieces, and look for a new glass? We need to accept the fact that to be confused, anxious, depressed, and even ill during these times is, for the most part, perfectly normal. We do have choices here. We can deny our reality, put on a positive face, get busy in the myriad of so-called senior activities today, and totally miss our call to enter the dark forest of ourselves and of our future where there are no paths. It is not so easy to turn our back on what everyone else is doing and what the people around us are expecting us to do.

It might be helpful for us to remember that primitive cultures faced the major transition periods in life as a society. They developed initiation ceremonies and rituals that supported their tribal members as they went through life's transitional periods and a period of symbolic death and rebirth into a new way of being and living. Everyone in the society participated in these rituals and supported the people going through these transformative situations. Their members too were scared and depressed before the ceremonies. We may need to consider that John's depression after retiring and Elizabeth's confusion and anxiety were perfectly normal and to be expected. These are not signs of weakness, neurosis, dysfunction, or failure. They are signs that we are facing major life changes.

We might also consider that, because our culture has developed such a mercenary and utilitarian attitude that demonstrates little empathy for our actual well-being, we are not going to get societal recognition and support during our transitional periods. I have come to recognize that psychotherapy and Jungian analysis are currently two of the best supportive containers to help us accept the call and go through the initiation process that can transform us as we transition into the fourth quarter of our lives. Of course, I realize that, as effective as these modalities can be, they aren't available to everyone. That is why I write my books and hope they will be helpful, healing, inspiring, and transforming for as many people as possible.

Knowledge can change our lives if we can put it to use and help one another with it. So my experience with my cancer and my deep reflections and dialogs with it (shared in my book *Radical Hope*) not only renewed my vocation, but also transformed my writing from what had been a private passion into a more urgent calling.

Becoming Engaged

We have split ourselves in a drastic way in our society. Even though we think we are very aware of our cultural problems, we may not be nearly as aware as we think we are. We have been brought up in the social character of our culture and have had many of these beliefs, values, and attitudes indoctrinated into us. We are like the proverbial frog that is put into a pan of water. Then the heat is slowly turned up until the frog is cooked and dead, without ever realizing what was happening or that it could have jumped out. Almost from birth, the split between our heads and hearts begins. Our school system is ruled by a doctrine of efficiency that, in effect, is so competitive that it becomes a system of learning based on humiliation.

Our parenting patterns follow suit, as we push our children to be more and better in school, on the playing field, and sometimes both. Parenting, too, becomes a subtle but strong push for children to be something other than what they are and "humiliation parenting," such as telling a child, "You should be ashamed of yourself" or "Couldn't you have gotten an *A* in that?" has become the norm. That is the beginning of the "heat" that is being turned up on us. Then we grow into a culture that is identity oriented and achievement oriented, that values outgoing, can-do-appearing people; concrete facts; rational thinking; and being objective, unemotional, and decisive.

As I wrote earlier, this perspective leaves us self-alienated, with little empathy for our own well-being (other than materially), for the actual well-being of others, and for cultivating our imagination. It also leaves us with a frame of mind that tends to dismiss our needs for self-knowledge, knowledge in general, and a passion for being alive. From this perspective, getting therapeutic help for a major life change and for building a new life is often criticized as wasting time, wasting money, navel-gazing, and becoming dependent.

■ ■ ■

The problem we face is that we are not living with divided hearts—we are living split off from our hearts. Since this "water" has been "heating" so slowly during our lives, we have not realized that we are in a desperate situation, personally as well as culturally. Even our helping professions aren't realizing the magnitude of the situation, as they focus on problem solving, medications, and "getting back to normal" when, in fact, we need to jump out of the boiling water of "normal." Every one of us needs to pause, to think, and to question how we are living. To jump out of the boiling water, to heal our relationship with our hearts so they can become key parts of the foundation of a new life requires a quest and an inner journey that begins by cultivating our knowledge and our experiences of our emotions.

■ ■ ■

The first step in engaging with our lives is understanding that it is our emotions that connect us directly to the vibrancy of life. Unless we are fully in touch with our emotions and anchored in the heart of who we truly are, our personality is like a tree without roots and does not have access to the deep inner energy that can strengthen and nourish us. In the process of our growth in the fullness of our lives, this inner rootedness becomes the source that revitalizes our permanent journey of growth and transformation. Tapping into and acknowledging these roots of our emotions provide the key to living a life of depth, imagination, and passion.

Our emotions are powerful, highly significant forces that can reveal problems, threaten us, paralyze us, and turn us into stone. They can also offer deep experiences of truthfulness, lift us up, animate us, and bring us into love and ecstasy. During major emotional and physical upheavals in my life, I have often been surprised and at times even frightened by the flood of feelings erupting in me. "Where do they come from?" I wonder. "And what do they mean? What kind of messengers are they?" As we begin to look at these essential questions, I would like to share a story with you from my experience.

Several years ago, Gary, a mild-mannered minister in his early sixties, came to see me. Gary was recovering from a heart attack and bypass surgery. I was surprised when he opened our meeting by saying, "I want to stop being a spectator of life." When I asked him if he could explain a little more about what he meant, he replied, "The terror of almost dying and being cut open may be the first time I've felt really alive in years. It woke me up. I realized that I think everyone else is living, but I've just been watching and going through the motions. For years I've just gotten up and done what needed to be done without thinking too much about it. Love, fear, excitement, enthusiasm, bitterness, illness, pain—those were all things I saw in other people's lives." Gary had come to understand that without feelings, our lives seem more like a movie we're watching than a process we're fully involved in.

Before his surgery, Gary said, he had actually considered himself a "feeling" person. He thought he loved the people close to him and cared about his work, and he added that sometimes he even cried at movies. He also admitted he had a bit of an anger problem, with occasional outbursts and moments of road rage. He didn't really see himself as emotionally inhibited nor did he consider that there might be an accumulation of unconscious anger behind the anger that would sometimes burst into his consciousness. So Gary was surprised when his wife and a couple of people close to him told him that he seemed angry all of the time. They also attested that he often seemed to remain passive in situations when he should have acted on legitimate feelings of anger and also in situations in which he was being put down.

Gary's wife, Janet, too, considered herself a "feeling" person and in touch with her own emotions. But she confessed that she was often uncomfortable or paralyzed by the emotions she regarded as taboo. She shared that when she was growing up, she had been taught there were "good" emotions like joy and sympathy and "bad" emotions like anger, fear, and depression. She was also taught that "bad" emotions were characteristics of a weak or dysfunctional person. So, as a result of her early teachings, she found that it threatened her self-esteem when she would experience or admit to experiencing these "bad" emotions. Earlier in her life, when she was in the sixth grade, in a moment of embarrassment when she was at the blackboard, little Janet had burst into tears. She was so humiliated that she didn't allow herself to cry again for more than forty years. Her first tear came when her daughter was in a serious automobile accident.

Many of us, to a greater or lesser extent, were taught or indoctrinated into developing a repressive style, like Gary or Janet, when facing any of our strong emotions. We were not encouraged to try to understand them, their origins, and their meaning. Being emotionally overwhelmed was often treated as a source of shame and embarrassment. And if it was compounded by tendencies toward being a perfectionist, an accommodator, sensitive, or feeling compelled to be good, then the experience was exacerbated by feelings of losing control, being rejected, and even of being attacked and humiliated, by our own inner critic, if no one else. We found out early on that being angry, expressing disappointment, withdrawing in sadness, and expressing other deeply felt expressions were considered childish and immature. So we adapted by attempting to avoid conflict, to keep the peace, and to shun "wasting energy" by being emotional. Because of this adaptation, we often became anesthetized and passive, with a paralysis of consciousness, in a state of defensive, intellectual lethargy.

For the most part, though, we are so unaware of these defenses against our emotions and our style of repressing them that, like Gary before his heart attack, we don't even notice our real feelings or distinguish them from our thoughts. In this pragmatic world we live in, the wisdom of our emotions is usually discounted, and we are instructed to avoid our emotions whenever we are making important decisions. Repressing our emotions then causes us to develop an inauthentic persona as well as a distorted value system. Being determined to control our emotions and our bodies also diminishes the connection to our heart and isolates us in our heads. Whether occurring from a recent event or from our childhood, repressed emotions live on, and it takes more and more energy to keep them under control. There is no timeline in our unconscious; emotions that have been repressed stay as alive as they were when they happened. It is no wonder then that passion, love, and purpose are not readily available to us, and that somewhere deep inside, our rebellious feelings continue to tell us that we are somehow betraying our true selves.

The way to strengthen our personality, our little self, is to learn how to truly experience our emotions. Pursuing self-knowledge and awareness then becomes the cornerstone for cultivating our relationship with our emotions. The emotions that we have repressed and re-garded as dark, irrational, threatening, and undesirable must now be brought into the light of our awareness and be recognized and accepted for the truth they reveal. Tucked behind these denied feelings are our wounds that need to be healed and our shadows, the parts of ourselves we have exiled in order to become acceptable and safe. These emotions, which are struggling to break into our awareness through many kinds of symptoms, are actually messengers telling us that there are aspects of ourselves longing to be found, longing to be recognized, to be-come active parts of who we are, and to heal the splits within us.

These are the feelings and potentials that opened Gary, Janet, John, Elizabeth, Cynthia, and myself to a new life. It is important to be willing to conscientiously pursue these feelings by reflecting upon our experiences and our emo-tional history. We must look for the emotions that are try-ing to become known, the ones we feel in our bodies, the ones in our dreams, and the ones that slip into our minds when we are half asleep, ruminating in our beds. This is the winding path to integrating our true feelings and to learn-ing how they can expand and inform us. The ambience of our lives and the richness of our relationships as well as our capacity to be passionate, loving, creative, and authentic as we move through life *all* depend upon our ability to listen to and support our emotional well-being.

Being able to feel deeply and knowing why we actually feel a particular way are our keys to understanding how engaged in life we really are. Our feelings help us to gauge how much we like or don't like something, how much we value or don't value something, whether something is congruent with who we really are, whether something diminishes us or supports and affirms us, and whether something or someone is violating our boundaries or affirming and respecting our personhood. Listening to and understanding our emotions help us stop mishandling our needs and those of the people we care about. It allows our "feeling function" (a Jungian term) or our emotional intelligence to provide "messages" so we can pay attention to our relationships and cultivate personal values that emphasize our whole being—head, heart, and hands—not just the pragmatic and conventional aspects. Tremendous energy then becomes available to us, which can daily strengthen and nourish us and help us feel safely rooted within ourselves. This energy becomes the key to our being fully engaged in life.

In this country we like to think of ourselves as champions of freedom. But we have to ask ourselves on a deep, personal level, "Are we really ready? Do we really want to be free?" To be really free, we must thoroughly know the depth and values of our hearts and the potential strengths, courage, and love that can live there. My hope for all of us is that through our emotions, we can rediscover how to shift our lives to living from our hearts. I hope that we can move the seat of our morality from our heads and their utilitarian approach to life to our hearts. I also hope that we can teach these values to our children and our grandchildren by being engaged in life.

3

Facing Dangerous Moments

Have you ever considered that we are facing a dangerous moment in our lives? In the previous chapter, I pointed out that we have been taken over by an attitude of materialism and utilitarianism without realizing that we are being reduced to sensation-seeking, passive onlookers. We are becoming spectators of the game of life. Our true passion for knowledge and our capacity to live from our hearts are slipping away from us like sand through our fingers. Our real capacity to be compassionate, even with ourselves, has faded into the background of our daily lives. The utilitarian mind-set that has taken over our world has also caused us to cynically dismiss our imagination. As a result, we live in an era when neither young nor old seem able to create a vision of themselves in a better world.

Advertising, the media, and profit-oriented institutions have learned how to create our visions of a better world for us and then sell them to us. For example, when

I see ads for retirement homes, I see smiling men and women sitting in boats on a pond, playing golf, or walking and chatting on well-manicured trails. This life looks inviting, and I am not against retirement homes. But I am suspicious about any version of the "good life" that some ad is trying to sell to me.

When Robert, the surgeon whom I mentioned earlier, retired and then began working in Africa, he said that for the first time in decades, he felt like his vocation had been renewed. Being out from under the cost and assembly-line pressures of American medicine allowed him to see and feel like he was truly making a difference in people's lives. Elizabeth, who became a pastoral counselor in her midsixties, also felt the satisfaction of a new vocation that helped people improve their lives. Cynthia reported similar satisfaction from her Peace Corps experiences. Their imagination of what it meant to be alive and engaged had become freed, and it took them far beyond the visions presented by the media.

There is also a darker side to the way we are collectively approaching aging and turning it into a new industrial complex. Atul Gawande explains this problem very well in his important book *Being Mortal*. You should read this book, and I won't try to summarize it because I couldn't do it justice in such a short space. But there are two things I would like to mention relating to this subject from my own professional experience that I think are worth thinking about, in even the best retirement homes.

First, Martha, a retired certified public accountant, asked me one day, "How would you like to live in an up-scale community where six to eight people died every month?" That is a question I consider every time I see one of those lovely ads. In another case, David, a retired physics professor living in an upscale retirement home, told me that he didn't believe in an afterlife. He thought that after we died, there was just the void, so why should he do anything other than seek comfort every day? These kinds of depressive outlooks are easily fostered by our overly rational, utilitarian approach to the material good life.

There are only two ways that I can think of to deal with these bleak perspectives. The first one is the inner quest that leads to the discovery of a self you did not know existed, a true experience of independence and new attitudes toward life and death. This approach leads us to the second solution to these attitudes. As we become engaged with ourselves on a more profound level, we will also become engaged with a new purpose and a new relationship to life itself.

This discussion reminds me of Huston Smith, the great religious scholar, who became so disabled by rheumatoid arthritis in his nineties that he could no longer be cared for at home. He had to go to an extended care facility. Within a short period of time, he was organizing classes in the world's religions for other people in the facility. Huston Smith had a passion for his calling, as well as the imagination and the vision to keep it alive as long as he was alive. Huston Smith, like the other people I've mentioned, is a pathfinder into a new way of truly maturing and aging strong. Our task is to learn from his example, to follow the inner quest to free or rediscover our potentials, our purpose, and then to create our own path. There are some dangers along the way, some pitfalls, and I want to explore three of them in the rest of this chapter.

A Plague of Disengagement

Jennifer Percy immediately caught my attention when she pointed out that America is suffering from a "plague of disengagement" in the *New York Times Book Review* on February 2, 2015. Jennifer describes our attitude toward our war veterans, saying we don't listen to them, how they were hurt; she concludes that we don't want to understand them. Of course this is a tragedy. But while reading her article and clenching my teeth in sadness and frustration, I was also thinking, "Are we any different with our prisoners, our poor, our mentally ill, our addicts, or our aging poor and middle class? What about our chronically ill, our children, our alienated teenagers?" We don't want to understand the wounded and, in Jungian terms, the shadow parts of our society. And if we are going to pay attention to Jung, isn't the heart of this problem centered in our unwillingness to seek to understand the wounded and shadow sides of ourselves? Jung is pretty clear when he writes, "The psychological rule says that when an inner situation is not made conscious, it happens outside as fate."

What impresses me, however, is the number of people my wife and I are encountering in our practices and presentations who are interested in knowing and transforming their lives. They are beginning to become engaged with the deeper significance of their lives and what it means to be human. But what really scares me is how many other people are adamantly defending their positions of disengagement. Perhaps I shouldn't be all that surprised, because Jung warned us that if we sincerely set out on this journey to become fully engaged and to know ourselves, it wouldn't be easy. The entire conventional shadow of our culture would oppose us, including its practical, intellectual, moral, and religious components. On the outside, we may be looked at as weird, different, self-centered, selfish, and so on. Internally, we may be wondering the same thing or hearing those voices that tell us we are not really worth all of the attention we are giving ourselves and that our investment of time and effort in being engaged isn't really worth it.

It may help us to remember another well-known quotation from Jung. In his BBC interview, he passionately says, "The world hangs by a slender thread, and that thread is the consciousness of man…We are the greater danger…What if something goes wrong with the psyche?…But we know nothing about it." And, he continues, it seems that, "If we are well fed and clothed, we have little urge to learn about ourselves—and that is our greatest mistake of all." In this case, we easily slide into a self-satisfied mediocrity of awareness and sensitivity that leaves us living with indifference to the deepest meaning of life.

In the face of this danger, real self-care only begins when we start the inner journey into self-knowledge and individuation. To avoid or refuse this inward journey causes our energies and our potentials to back up into our shadows and what we are learning to call our "unlived lives." Eventually, the repressed energies in our unlived lives turn sour and even dark. As the avoidance of this process continues, we may become more rigid, emotionally defensive, and afraid of risks and begin to see life as threatening and the future as lacking promise. At this point, we are beginning to lose our souls—to become soul-sick—and we may find ourselves getting physically sick as well.

When we are listening to the news or other people, we may wonder why the advocates of different factions in our society seem so angry, so fanatic, and so threatened that they are actually nullifying life while claiming to be promoting our best interests. Fanaticism; self-righteousness; and the anger, fear, and aggressiveness that accompany them are the symptoms of our soul-sickness, whether on the political right or left, in the center, or on the fringes. As Massimilla and I wrote the section on "Facing the Death Mother" in our recent book *Into the Heart of the Feminine: Facing the Death Mother Archetype to Reclaim Love, Strength, and Vitality*, our understanding of our "plague of disengagement" as a consequence of the wounded and repressed feminine in our lives became increasingly clear.

We quote the Jungian analyst and author Marion Woodman as she writes, "The Death Mother wields a cold, fierce, violent, and corrosive power. She is rampant in our society right now." This is the face our society turns toward our war veterans, people who have lost their jobs, poor mothers, the poor in general, the chronically ill, prisoners, and yes, many of us who are older. This is the face we have learned to turn toward our own struggles, failures, vulnerabilities, disappointments, fading dreams, and other challenges. Through fear and self-criticism, we learn from the Death Mother to live too conservatively, too defensively, to not take risks and that, if we throw ourselves wholeheartedly into life, we may end up looking ridiculous or losing everything. This book reflects much of our own journeys of seeking, step-by-step, to become fully engaged in our lives.

As we have lived with my daughter and her experiences of progressive multiple sclerosis since 2006, we have had to relearn how cold our country's health care system is in failing to even want to understand the financial and emotional costs of being in such a condition. Nor do we, as a culture, want to understand any of the other struggling aspects of being human that I have mentioned or, as Jung said, to understand ourselves, as long as we are well fed and clothed. But even though, as a culture, we reflect coldness and disengagement, my daughter has found a very caring and supportive community of family and friends. And we have found people in our practices, lectures, workshops, and the groups we speak to who are looking for ways to become engaged; to open their hearts; and to return the strength, love, and creativity of the feminine to our lives.

So, in spite of our "plague of disengagement," Massimilla and I have hope. We also are hopeful that our books will help people open their hearts and reclaim their lives, as living into a book's creation helps us. Seeing people willing to open themselves and change their lives strengthens our hope that together we can shake our society out of its willful amnesia—its denial of the greater aspects of being human, the beauty and the horror of the life we all live.

When Dreams Die: Becoming Stronger at Our Broken Places

By the time we reach our age, we all have had dreams that die. We have dreamed how we want our lives to be and who we wanted to become. Many of us dreamed of creating a family better than our original one. And we dreamed of being able to share our love in better ways than our early models showed us.

We may still dream of success, good health, safety, security, love, and warmth—of knowing and being known, of being heard, recognized, and appreciated. We often have dreams for our children, our future, and our creativity. We have little dreams and big dreams, and sometimes we just dream of life being kind, gentle, and just. But what happens to us when our dreams fail? Of course the failure of the bigger dreams that we have invested our hearts in is more challenging than the failure of our smaller dreams.

I've always found it helpful, especially when I'm facing failure, to have a map in mind for the journey that I am facing. So let us look at the failure of bigger dreams. What does it do to us when the marriage or relationship that we had so much hope for fails? What does it do to us if a child or loved one dies? Or if a business is shipwrecked? Or if we are diagnosed with a serious illness? How does it affect us when we finally realize the mother and father we spent our lives trying to please never loved us and never will or that their love was broken and destructive to our souls?

These thoughts remind me of Ernest Hemingway's hauntingly beautiful passage in *A Farewell to Arms*, where he writes, "If people bring so much courage to this world, the world has to kill them to break them, so of course it kills them. The world breaks every one and afterward, many are strong at the broken places. It kills the very good and the very gentle and the very brave impartially. If you are none of these, you can be sure it will kill you too, but there will be no special hurry." To dream of a better life at any age engages us in being fully alive and shows our deepest longing for a more desirable life. It takes the courage Hemingway is talking about to be really engaged in our lives, to hope, to risk, and to try with all of our hearts. Being fully engaged requires that we dream, and if our dream dies, due to our unrealistic expectations or a cruel twist of fate, how can we become stronger at our broken places?

We should also ask ourselves, "What does *broken* really mean?" Allowing ourselves to be broken is the hardest part of this journey because of our culture's emphasis on positive thinking, achievement, and happiness. We live in a world where admitting our pain and weaknesses is seen as an admission of failure.

Long before I dreamed of becoming a Jungian analyst, Dr. Jung's writings guided me through some of my darkest periods and into a new life. Dr. Jung explains that when our life collapses, it "feels like the end of the world, as though everything has tumbled back into the original chaos." He then gives us three alternatives as to how to face these situations—situations in which dreams have died.

To begin with, we may become overwhelmed by circumstances and events. Then, we may just give up, literally and figuratively die, and sleepwalk through the balance of our lives, never risking truly becoming who we have the potential to be. Secondly, we may cling to the images of our old lives, trying our best to reclaim the vestiges and attitudes of those former lives. We may prop up the facade of our former "normalcy." I have seen too many people insist on keeping up the appearances of a positive attitude no matter what the loss or illness was. I believe people in this group become, in Hemingway's words, people who are killed with "no special hurry."

Our third and best alternative is to begin the journey that will open us up to hearing and understanding the inner voice that can help us become "stronger at the broken places." With a commitment to this third choice, we enter the classic hero or heroine's quest, the night-sea journey, the dark night of the soul, the voyage that has been called by so many names. We must all take this voyage if we are going to find our capacity to dream again, find a deeper purpose in our lives and a new myth (a new structure of values and meaning) to live by. We must be prepared to walk through the hell of suffering and passion, through our subjection to the emotional and spiritual crucible in which transformation takes place, in order for us to become stronger at the broken places.

This journey begins with the receptive qualities we find by embracing the natural features of the archetypal feminine. And, as always, this embrace includes accepting our life, which doesn't mean surrendering to it. We must become still and go down into ourselves, our unconscious, as the ancient Sumerian Goddess Inanna went on her mythological journey into the underworld. We must honor the muted consciousness of the night and the moonlight and ponder our lives and situations in our hearts.

For me, this means quieting my strong, active personality—my ego—and put it in the position that T. S. Eliot shares with us when he writes that we must let the darkness come upon us, as if we are in a theater waiting for a scene to be changed. As I sit in the embrace of the archetypal feminine, I am there for transformation and not for mothering, trying to become more open to my inner voice through an attitude of spiritual waiting, tending to life's essentials, and cultivating a readiness for listening for that voice. I am also carefully paying attention to my nightly visits from my unconscious. As my old dreams die, so does my old identity, and during this process I become reacquainted with my deeper hungers and longings to be loved, to experience the Divine, and to know my life has meaning and is valuable and that I can find a measure of peace and satisfaction. It is while I am in this state that I can begin to experience my bigger Self, the greater personality within me that supports me and creates a new life.

Through these difficult ordeals, I begin discovering the true meaning of *religio*, which is relating back to a power greater than my everyday personality. Enduring the journey and the suffering that opens us to our depths joins us to the greater story of humanity and our greater Self. We become connected to this divine center that will help us be born anew and will accompany us through the flames of our pain, disappointments, and grief. This journey becomes the foundation for helping us find a new purpose and direction in our lives that are true expressions of the essence of who we are becoming.

But I want to note that when some dreams die, when some things are lost, we will need to find a special chamber or chapel for them in our hearts. This will be a very special place where we honor our loss and grief and carry them in our hearts for as long as we live.

As I have lived, loved, and worked, this has been the essence of the process by which I discovered the true meaning in Dr. Jung's words: "For we are in the deepest sense, the victims and the instruments of cosmogonic love." It is also how I have become stronger at the broken places.

The Danger in Our Unlived Lives

Our "unlived lives," which we may have accumulated over decades, take their revenge through our restless feelings of dissatisfaction, guilt over failing to live up to our hopes and dreams, emotional pain that undermines us, destructive habits, and even in our illnesses. The roots of the things that often disrupt our lives, drain our energy, and thwart our intentions lie in the conflict between our longings for growth and freedom, our longings for peace and safety, and our reluctance or refusal to pay the price for our authenticity through a special kind of suffering. In *The Age of Anxiety*, W. H. Auden says, "We would rather be ruined than changed. We would rather die in our dread than climb the cross of the moment and let our illusions die."

The special kind of suffering I am talking about comes when we try our best to acknowledge the psychological and emotional issues that drive our lives, to seek to transform them, and to live the unlived portions of our lives that have been left in their wake. We call this "transformative suffering." This venture will quickly teach us that to love life and to be fully engaged in it will threaten the walls supporting the identity we have so carefully constructed. The major transition periods in our adult lives, such as the one at midlife and the one when we are entering the fourth quarter, are natural times for the unlived aspects of ourselves to try to rise to the surface. Whether you choose to accept this challenge or not determines the potential health and fulfillment in your future. One of the greatest dangers you may face in these periods is believing that who you are, where you are, and what you have in your current perspective are all there is. One of the primary missions of your big Self is to help you become the most complete and vital version of yourself.

Most of us want to define ourselves as some version of a person who wants to think positively; is nice, good, and caring; handles money well; takes obligations seriously; and generally acts responsibly. In fact, to even begin questioning how we have defined ourselves and seeking to become more conscious of our wholeness creates a fear that we may be only dimly aware of but is as strong as our fear of death. In addition, far too many of us feel so overwhelmed by our obligations and the pace of our lives that we only long for peace and balance. To be in this position makes Dr. Jung's statement that "he could not imagine a fate more awful, a fate worse than death—than a life lived in perfect balance and harmony" both baffling and scary.

The creation story of our unlived lives starts soon after we are born, as we begin shaping ourselves to avoid shame, punishment, harm, and embarrassment. Little daily decisions and bargains with ourselves help us become collaborators in the demise of our spirits. Choosing how we will be good, what we will rebel against, the desirability of certain playmates, bribes for grades, or good grades to earn love, help us sell out our integrity and undermines our self-worth, even though some of this is necessary to actually form our identity and grow up. Embracing practicality, being sensible, the promise of a good life with success and the avoidance of pain keep us off the byways that could add depth, meaning, and vitality to our lives. The inner voices of integrity, conscience, and authenticity weaken against the pressure of conventional wisdom, busy and demanding lives, and the fearful appearance of the world. Before long, we are so embedded in our identities that, without our knowing it, what we have considered our best characteristics may have become expressions of our major psychological complexes. Yet questioning ourselves has become difficult and threatening, as we fear that it may disrupt our lives.

To reverse this process in order to become more whole and authentic, we must find the courage to face the parts of ourselves we have denied. The process actually begins with confronting our ideals, values, and obligations. In the long run, our options may be to confront them or to die from them. I have seen more than one person sacrifice his or her life to an illness rather than give up the persona of a positive attitude and take the perilous journey into grief, rage, and history. It is no easy matter to consider that our melancholy, despair, rage, and fear may be the gateways to new life, creativity, love, and awe.

I remember working with a woman who had been brought up as the youngest of four children by a cold mother and an angry father. She survived her childhood by doing well in school and later by pleasing her superiors. But in midlife her denied needs and potentials rebelled, leaving her overweight and depressed. The answer for her was not in the mainstream treatment of her depression. It was in getting to know the internalized foundation of negativity that kept her so self-critical and self-belittling that an important part of her was paralyzed by passivity. Working through this complex freed her animus, her inner masculine strength that could support her having her own voice. Psychologically, it was like Cinderella breaking free to meet her prince. This prince helped her recognize her denied capacities and gave her the strength to devote her life to bringing these abilities into her living reality.

I also recall a man in his midfifties who had been raised to be a pleaser, to repress the strength of his own desires, and to sublimate his needs into finding approval by satisfying others. But after two failed marriages, he realized that his relationships had been formed on a lie, a version of himself that wasn't deeply real, and on an idealism that would make any relationship hopeless. To begin with, he had to find the courage to face disapproval, to take the risks of first standing up to the voices of indoctrination in his psyche, and then to confront the people his new identity disturbed. This group included the people he had unconsciously trained to expect him to be a pleaser. Then, in order to free his anima, to allow his inner Cinderella to come to the ball, he had to explore his moods, the ones he had tried to conceal even from himself, along with the blocked emotions they represented.

In these two oversimplified examples, both people had to face the fear and loneliness that had pressured them into their roles and then their anger and grief over their early reality. This vital work released new, potent energy within them and increased their feelings of strength, competence, and hope in the future.

Our unlived lives—the values, visions, talents, and longings we haven't admitted—are actually necessary as part of our wholeness and essential to support our true purpose, meaning, and trust in life. Unlived life will begin rebelling when its repression becomes a toxic part of our makeup and when our failure to love ourselves is failing our future.

This rebellion will test us in the halls of the most sacrosanct and vulnerable parts of how we value ourselves, the foundations of our identity. Facing ourselves and our unlived lives isn't easy work. We call it "confronting the shadow," but the need for it shows that we are being called by the life force within our depths, the big Self, to truly experience a second birth, to become a cocreator with the Divine, and to live beyond our conventional ideas of the good life, in order to help heal and redeem ourselves and our part of the world.

Our greatest spiritual traditions are based on the themes of self-knowledge, growth, and transformation. The continuous search for self-knowledge brings us clarity and an ease of decision making. We know who we are. We know what we are here for, what matters most, and what matters least. Then, when we say yes, it is strong and enthusiastic, and when we say no, it is firm and resolute. The mystical traditions raise our journey into wholeness to a journey into holiness. This lifts our lives into a realm that is far more profound than simply trying to be good and happy. The call of our unlived life is a call from our big Self. The big Self, in Jungian terms, you may recall, represents our instinctual drive for consciousness and wholeness. Archetypically, it is the supreme ordering system in our psyche and is continuously focused on trying to develop us to fulfill the highest potentials within us. The real struggle is between our willingness to participate in our transformation and our often unconscious yearning to stay safely grounded in our old selves.

The failure to search for the calls of the Self in the midst of my struggles and the avoidance of the encounters that reveal them are risks I am no longer willing to take. Whether these events fail to enrich my life or bring it new hope, joy, and love along with life's suffering is up to me. The cross of the moment may require me to overcome my dread or lethargy with passion, and if I do so, the moment of the special suffering of transformation will give birth to hope, confidence, and the renewed experience of being fully alive—the most alive I have ever felt, even as I approach my eighth decade.

4

Bringing Our Lives Together

A few years ago, I met Kitty, a well-dressed, intelligent woman in her seventy-sixth year. Her family was grown, and her husband was a senior partner in a large law firm in a major city. They had moved to the area to retire. However, her husband decided he wasn't ready to retire and continued to commute four days a week to his law practice. Sitting quietly across from me in my office, Kitty explained that she wanted to tell me the whole story of her life. Early in our conversation, she shared with me that she suffered from Crohn's disease. She was sure it first manifested itself while she was in high school, but it had gone undiagnosed for many years and had caused her and her family a lot of suffering. Kitty began her story by telling me about her parents and her birth.

She told her story slowly, trying to resurrect every detail that she could. She was especially interested in uncovering more about her childhood years. Kitty knew there were years where a lot happened in her family's life, but her memories of those periods were either blank or fragmented. In our initial conversation, she made it clear that she didn't care how long this process took. She then added that she wanted me to listen very carefully as she tried to cover her life thoroughly and then to help her put it together.

Seeing our lives as stories is an important perspective for me, and I was both honored by and very interested in joining Kitty in this undertaking. The process lasted for a little over seven months. Kitty's story, with all of its ups and downs, and the background of the pain of her illness became the context in which she accepted the entirety of her life and gained a sense of peace and new respect for herself. When our stories are personal, they become much more than entertaining fantasies. They are like a spiral staircase. We can go down the stairs into the past that we are connected to and almost always come back up with a better understanding of ourselves. We can pause on the level of the present and gain new insight into it. Then, as we link our insights from the present to our new understandings of the past, we can envision our lives as they are becoming. Sometimes we have to go down the staircase and deep into the basement of the past in order to be able to unlock the future we have been trying to climb to.

Thinking about stories always reminds me of the classic myths and fairy tales that I have loved for most of my life. They are full of fear, struggle, hopelessness, and humiliation that have to be experienced before confidence, love, and joy can be won as the rewards for persevering; enduring; surviving hardships, big and small; and remaining true to ourselves. By carefully developing and listening to our stories as Kitty did, we may be amazed at how much we suffered and struggled. We may find our confidence renewed, our passion reenergized, our purpose strengthened, and our ability to accept life and desire enlarged. When we can really face and accept our pain, we become much less susceptible to the ease and safety promised by our marketing establishment. When we can truly learn to accept our pain and also see some of the humorous aspects of our lives, we become much more open to love and joy. Then, if we take our time and pay careful attention to our stories, we can begin to detect that there have been unseen, guiding hands influencing the way our stories have been taking place. We may imagine that this has been the influence of the big Self directing and supporting our journey through life. And I must admit that I have, at times, wished this guiding hand had chosen another, gentler way to direct me and that, at times, I wouldn't have minded having an easier path.

Somewhere along the way into our fourth quarter of life, we all seem to have a natural urge to do what Kitty did. Many of the people I've known wanted to write their stories, or write stories from their lives, or arrange their photo albums by year, or record some of their life events for their grandchildren. I always urge people to do this, to get busy at it. It can bring us a lot of satisfaction to put our lives into this kind of context. In the next few pages, I'm going to share some simple thoughts about the Jungian process of seeing life and dreams through the lens of story. The fourth quarter is a natural and important time in our lives to expand our imagination this way to help us feel more at home in the complexity of our lives and experiences.

The Jungian Process: Story, Dreams, Healing, and Fulfilling our Lives

As we move into the fourth quarter of our lives, it is helpful if we look at the importance of the concept of story in Jungian psychology. We can also look at the importance of the idea of story—our story and the greater story of humanity—and our knowledge of our story in particular in developing self-awareness and bringing our lives to wholeness and their full expression.

In olden times, we created culture by using stories to give a sense of form and meaning to life, to give us a sense of the mysteries of life, and to connect us to those mysteries. Today, we tell our children stories to entertain and to teach them. They in turn hunger for the eternal themes in stories that connect them to life's mysteries. The current popularity of the Percy Jackson books that connect children with the Divine—he is the son of Poseidon and a mortal woman—and to the hero myth, as the characters develop and fight evil, is a good example.

All of our great wisdom traditions and religions are made up of stories that teach. And we are struggling to reimagine these stories so they can help inform our lives. Many of us have had the experience that, when we began a relationship with a lover, our intimacy was initiated as we shared our stories with each other. Stories connect us with each other, with important values, and with patterns of living that give meaning and healing, and they connect us with the transcendent aspects of life, as well as our deeper selves. A real story touches the mind, the heart, and the soul.

Yet we are living in a world that is destructive to our experience of stories. Television gives us disconnected news blips, soap operas, sitcoms, and reality shows that have no deeper theme, while everything is fragmented by the insertion of commercials. And talk radio has no story to tell us, as it only tries to arouse emotions. Movies like *Avatar* turn archetypal themes into emotional entertainment and rob these themes of their truly transformative power. This cultural direction has caused us to develop a resistance to "story" in its more profound forms. The hum of noise, often referred to as white noise, urges us to want security, the status quo, or to stop the world and get off. The world supports our resistance to stories, because to pay attention to them takes time.

I began my Jungian experience, as I have said, in the same way that many people did, by reading Dr. Jung's autobiography, *Memories, Dreams, Reflections*. Every time I've reread this book, and I've done so many times, I have been struck in my own inner work and in my professional work when Dr. Jung writes, "The patient who comes to us has a story that is not told and which, as a rule, no one knows of. To my mind, therapy only really begins after the investigation of that wholly personal story. It is the patient's secret, the rock against which he [or she] is shattered."

Dr. Jung continues, "The problem is always the whole person, never the symptom alone. We must ask questions which challenge the whole personality." In other words, symptoms arise from this blockage of our story, and we must discover this story in order to have our life follow a track of authenticity, meaning, and fulfillment. Of course, every time I read this passage, I wonder anew what story I am living. Is it my real story, or is it a cover story that protects me, helps me fit in, and makes my life look like it's working?

Here are a few questions you might find helpful to ask yourself:

1. Am I living in my story?
2. Am I living a cover story?
3. How has this idea of Jung affected me?
4. What feelings came up when I read that we all have a secret story?
5. What feelings came up when I read that this may be the rock that blocks me or shatters my hopes and dreams?

Dreams and Story

It might surprise you to hear that, in Jungian psychology, we think every dream is a story or has a story behind it. In order to understand a dream, we try to understand it as a story and to understand what it is like for us and the characters in the dream to be in that particular story. So as we look at dreams, we look at classic dream structure:

1. the opening place and situation—the beginning
2. the complications, the flow of action, the complications that occur, or the lack of action
3. the climax of the action—the situation that is a turning point
4. the result—what has been solved, pointed out, or left unsolved

In other words, we look at the dream from the standpoint of classic dramatic structure. This perspective—the dream as a story—helps its flow of events make sense. For example, the dream opens, and I am in my childhood home. As I write my thoughts about and associations to the dream and its images, I will write about what it felt like to be in my childhood home, and I will wonder why or how I am still in this boyhood situation. As I go through my dream this way, one sentence or image at a time, I will be amplifying the dream into a broader story, and I will also become more personally informed by its story. Dreams remind us to pay attention to the stories of our lives, and they connect us to these stories. Here are some aspects to consider:

> Dreams with *shadow figures* in them—same-sex figures other than ourselves—are picturing unacknowledged characteristics, either good or bad, that are in ourselves, and they are telling us stories about our identities.

> Dreams with *anima or animus figures* in them are telling us stories about our relationship to ourselves and our relationships with others. Dr. Jung considered that each personality contains an image of the opposite sex. In other words, the

anima (or inner feminine image) is in the man's personality, and the animus (or inner masculine image) is in the woman's personality. The anima and animus images appear in dreams and in fantasies, and are projected onto individuals of the opposite sex, most often when we fall in love. This element in our own personality can be an inner guide and offers many creative possibilities in our journey of self-knowledge, so our inner relationship to it is very important.

Dreams with *archetypal images*—images that reflect great mythological or religious themes— in them speak about destiny, transformation, deep healing, and other soul issues. Almost every dream, if we develop it sufficiently, will usually come to a deeper theme, an archetypal pattern.

Seeing Our Life as a Story

If we live life as story, then we must remember that our childhood is not something that was simply good or wounding, but rather, it is the beginning of our story. In that regard, it is like a wellspring that we go back to, not as a source of pathology but as a source of new life. Our soul-self is our full being: body, mind, spirit, symptoms, fear, love, hurt, expectations, dreams, and fantasies. Many of our problems result from our ego getting scared and trying to use power to repress and overrule the biddings of our instincts and the desires of our hearts or hiding from powerful emotions like fear, shame, and rage.

Remembering that life as story is easier for our little self—our ego—to comprehend, because our flow of experiences can be seen in the context of a form, a structure that helps make sense of them. It is the limiting or blocking of our personal stories by ourselves, others, and our culture, and the nature of our environment that has tragic consequences. Our symptoms—physical and emotional—can show us how our story is limited. The question then becomes, "Can we change our story, our fate?" The answer is yes. Here are seven steps I want to share with you for changing your story:

Seven Steps for Changing and Reconstructing Your Story

1. See your wounds as having more meaning than you realized.
    The first thing is to accept our wounds and the emotional disturbances they caused as meaningful in some way. We need to let our old, locked-up interpretations around them die, so they can become the vehicles through which our deeper stories can emerge.
2. Step outside of the culture's plot.
    Then it is important to step out of the limitations that are imposed on these stories by the conventional

wisdom of our families and society, as well as to step beyond the expectations, fear, and shame these groups use to limit us.

3. Allow a new story to emerge.

We must then be willing to hold the tension between the elements in our old version of our story and the change taking place and endure the anxiety, while a new, deeper story is emerging into our lives.

4. Participate consciously in your story. Become a full actor in it.

It is important to consciously participate in this emergence by activating our imagination and creativity and becoming a full actor in our story.

5. Accept the creative cycle of life: life-death-rebirth.

Acknowledging and accepting the full creative cycle of life, death, and rebirth helps us get a true perspective of the greater reality. It is important to realize that we usually experience the death aspect of this process as conflict, betrayal, and disappointment. Keep in mind that remembering and accepting this full creative process is beyond normal in a society that sells the "good life."

6. Follow the soul contract.

Being in touch with our soul contract is our way of building self-awareness and personal consciousness and fueling our transformation. Here are practices for pursuing this journey:

a. Fully engage in life. Get beyond seeing life as something we want to avoid. Realize that taking risks, loneliness, conflict, defeat, and suffering are not only vital parts of life, they are also necessary to transformation, wholeness, and the experience of joy.

b. Take time to reflect upon your life. Be aware of the contradictions and struggles that come up in your life; don't ignore or repress them. Explore them and amplify your understanding of them. Bring the opposites into your full consciousness and hold them in your awareness. Use your journal, dreams, and active imagination to help you in this way. (See my book *Sacred Selfishness* for a fuller explanation.)

c. Bear the burden of conflict. It is important to realize, as Dr. Jung points out, that suffering is part of life; it is not pathological. It is our refusal to bear legitimate suffering that causes neurotic pain. So don't resort to "fight or flight" or to taking the easy way out or to trying to sublimate or repress the conflict.

d. Live the transformation. Remember, it is important to live the change, to live your story of being an expression of expanded consciousness,

self-awareness, and purpose. Otherwise, all this work is just a mind game.
7. Realize new influences.
   Finally, being awake to new influences that come to bear on our life and trusting the emergence of our new, deeper story are at the heart of this journey.

This whole process of life as story becomes healing and flows into our ongoing developmental process. We begin to recognize that we are in our own unique story of self-realization and the expression of the potential person we are meant to be. For all of this to happen, our ego, our little self, must become a committed seeker, or we will continue to be caught in a story that never evolves and is unable to fully engage in the love and fullness of life. What I have been telling you is a real distillation of Jungian theory and is beyond our culture's idea of normal.

■ ■ ■

Kitty discovered, as I did in writing part of my story in my book *Cracking Open*, that our stories are enlivened by the details, insights, and associations that flesh them out, take them deeper, enlarge their perspective, and relate them to the deeper flow of life. The Jungian ideas are meant to help us do the same thing. As we become more authentic, we become more of what really matters to us.

Our identity comes forth out of the mists of our changing lives through our memories, events, evolving images, hopes, and the profound feelings from our hearts. What I have found is that my life is a story that I am always discovering and shaping, where sometimes I lead, sometimes I follow, and sometimes I believe my story is writing me.

5

Harnessing the Strength of
Our Needs and Desires

I magine that your life is threatened, and in order to escape the threat, you must create another identity, a false cover. In a way, this is what most of us do as we grow up and seek to fit into the world. All too often, we think this false cover—this false cover story—is who we really are. But in reality, there is much more inside of us than we have included in our disguise, and these parts are crying out to be recognized.

Deep beneath the systems of order in our organized lives, stormy forces are often at work. We see these forces in Elizabeth's story, before she went through her transformation, at age sixty, into her new vocation as a pastoral counselor. Elizabeth came from a life that seemed ideal from an everyday perspective, and yet it became the example I would use of a woman's direct encounter with what we have called the Death Mother—the seat of these negative voices within us that we may be familiar with.

As we have been thinking about stories, we may also remember that mythical kingdoms symbolize the deeper forces in our personalities, such as Inanna's tempestuous journey into the underworld or our glimpses into Greek mythology's underworld, with its passionate lord, Hades, and his bride, Persephone, who preside over the kingdom of the past and the ghosts of our ancestors. Fairy tales show us the stories of violent fathers, sick kings, absent queens, stepmothers, dwarfs, heroes, and magical creatures, all carrying on lives in our unconscious that parallel the daily lives of our conscious personalities. These little kingdoms of alternative consciousness, emotions, values, and ideas maintain their existence, often waiting for us to search them out and become aware of the tremendous power they may be wielding in our emotional processes, relationships, and the directions of our lives.

Dr. Jung developed an approach that lends clarity and organization to our study of the unconscious and the forces that move us. He described the foundation of these forces in his work on complexes, those emotionally laden states of mind that come over us. He used myths and fairy tales to help us understand how these complexes are formed, how they act, and how they can be transformed and integrated into our inner work.

Frequently, we try as hard as we can to live in a "normal" state of maturity, as defined by the conventional models of existence we learned from our families and society. Or we try to rebel against these models, seeking a more fulfilling way of life that we are unable to attain because we have not yet faced the reality that shaped us, hurt us, dominated us, and is still blocking our path, like an avalanche on a mountain trail. Let us return to the story of Elizabeth for a moment. When Elizabeth reached middle age and was trying to live a conventional life or to rebel against the cold propriety and expectations of her mother, expectations she had long ago internalized, she ended up weeping and weeping, and the more she wept, the more furious she became at herself and at life. Something deep inside her was calling out for recognition and healing.

As we recognize our painful inner voices, it will comfort us to remember that the healing purpose of learning to understand ourselves in more profound, heartfelt ways isn't just to resolve our conflicts or to deal with our neuroses. Our deeper purpose is to join forces with the well of life and renewal within us. Individuation, as Jung called this process, connects us to the source of our evolving strength, wisdom, love, and other potentials. By embarking on this inner journey, we begin accepting our reality, healing ourselves, and opening the door to our true capacities for living. And please, please, remember one thing. We are never too old to take this journey and join forces with the well of life and renewal within us. For more than twenty years, I have seen amazing transformations and regenerations taking place in people in their mid to late eighties.

Elizabeth was frightened and ashamed of her tendency to break down in tears in front of other people. She was shocked at the vehemence of the exclamations that poured out of her in her analyst's office. Choking back her tears, she said, "I just can't do it anymore. I can't get my life together. I don't like myself. I hate the way I look. I hate looking crazy. I feel stupid, and the harder I try to...fix things, the worse it gets." When Elizabeth stopped blaming only herself, she was able to begin explaining her anger about her parents.

Previously, she had been directing her anger and fury inward, faulting herself for not being lovable and for not living up to her parents' expectations. Yet Elizabeth had been unaware of how much she was blaming herself. She had resented her mother's relentless expectations, which always seemed to exceed anything Elizabeth could achieve. Elizabeth's experiences with her mother's coldness and disdain had left her furious and had sabotaged her capacity to give and receive love. She was also devastated by her father's absence in general and his complicity with her mother when he was present. Bit by bit, Elizabeth began to realize that what looked like a childhood supplied with the "right stuff" was actually full of damaging events that had fashioned the plot of her life's story so far.

As Elizabeth learned more about herself, she began to grudgingly respect her rage and despair as turning points that forced her to begin the efforts to open up her life, to heal, and to grow, rather than to give up.

■ ■ ■

This brief example shows that as we grow up, we have to split off many of our personal characteristics and potentials in order to fit into our families, schools, and society. These parts of ourselves are then repressed and held in our unconsciousness, becoming what Jungians call our *shadow*. In our culture, we are also taught to repress our emotions, especially the stronger ones like fear, anger, sadness, and despair. This stifling of genuine emotion leaves us alienated from our whole or authentic personality potentials.

When our early lives are rough and challenging, abusive, or unloving and isolating, we are going to repress most of our emotions in order to feel safe and not to feel any more overwhelmed than we already are. As adults, whenever stressful events come up in our lives, these old reactive patterns will take over in our psyches and in our brains. In addition, we will have developed a psychological pattern of living that will be designed to protect us from the effects of events like those in our early lives, even though they are no longer a threat. A repressive, defensive style of living has become structured into our personality.

The primary reason for this is that the old emotions we repressed as children are still alive in our psyches and patterned in our brains. When a child grows up under difficult circumstances, that child will build up a large reservoir of anger or fear or both. It is important to remember there is no timeline in our unconscious. That reservoir of anger and/or fear will rest deep inside of us like a volcano until some event triggers an explosion.

Keeping these emotions repressed robs us of our vitality. Repressing our emotions takes a lot of energy. The cost to us is living with a constant amount of hypervigilance, anxiety, fatigue, and depression that may have gone on so long that we are no longer aware of then. In addition, repression leaves us emotionally encapsulated and unable to fully participate in loving relationships to the extent that we really want and need to. Eventually, the repressed energy in these emotions may become manifested in addictions, psychological and physical symptoms, and illnesses. Simply becoming aware of these emotions and expressing them is not the answer. If we avoid reexperiencing how we felt and how these patterns continue and merely talk about them from a safe distance, nothing changes in either our psyche or our neural pathways, and we have created a new defensive structure.

The true healing of these problems is to go beneath the surface of our conscious minds, enter into the unconscious, and explore our emotional wounds and experiences from within our emotional selves. By entering into the depth of our shadows, we are going into our emotions, the patterns they take, and the expressions that lie beneath our conditioning and beyond our conscious awareness. The emotions lead us to the heart of the problem and the patterns of behavior that they now evoke which we call, in Jungian terms, *complexes*. These patterns are also reflected in our neural pathways.

Transforming these patterns transforms our lives. This work can be helped by a Jungian analyst who is trained in depth work and has done this work himself or herself. This work of transformation is hard, necessary, and rewarding. But we have to work at it in the same committed way we would train for a marathon. We build up the emotional fitness for this work gradually through hard, personal work and emotionally lived experiences.

These following methods can be helpful and life changing when they become a devoted part of transforming your life:

Journaling: A great deal of research now shows that keeping a daily journal about ourselves, our thoughts, our feelings, and our concerns promotes good physical and emotional health. Journaling reflects our daily lives back to us and allows us to glimpse parts of ourselves we've hidden and our emotional responses to daily events and opens a field of perspective where our unconscious can emerge and our relationships to ourselves can become stronger. Our journals can also become the places for recording our dreams, fantasies, stories, and the other exercises I will suggest.

Acceptance: We must be open to accepting the emotions, thoughts, and memories that come up. We must also write them in our journals. This puts them into a concrete form, helps clarify them, and helps us relate to them more objectively. We give them expression by writing them down. They may also be expressed in other forms, such as art, sculpture, dance, and so on. These forms of expression may bring a sense of emotional release, but they are not transformative of the psychological patterns in our psyches and brains. These expressions must be carefully discussed with your analyst for real changes to take place.

Stories: We must tell the stories of our original wounding, our driven journeys, and our misguided attempts to find healing. And we must avoid telling them from an intellectual viewpoint, like a patient's history. We must tell the stories from inside our emotional selves.

The Helpful Analyst or Therapist: Transformation can lead to a whole new life. But it depends upon transforming the psychological patterns in our complexes and restructuring the emotional brain itself through building new neural networks. If you are afraid of being overwhelmed by your emotions, it will be very helpful to find a good Jungian analyst or therapist trained in Jungian psychology who understands the emotional depths in the shadow and the complexes they make up. Jungian psychology provides a context and structure for emotionally focused inner work with an empathetic analyst who has made this journey herself or himself. Transforming the neural patterns occurs primarily through the nonverbal, right-brain, implicit connection between the analyst or therapist and the client.

Helpful Questions for Reflecting and Journaling:

1. What kinds of things cause me stress?
2. What makes you angry or enraged?
3. What scares you and makes you feel vulnerable and insecure?
4. What do you worry the most about?

5. Who are the people who didn't treat you as well as you would have liked during your entire life? Start at the beginning.
6. What kind of stress affects you the most?
7. What kind of pain do you experience, and what connections does it have to your emotions?

Reflect on these questions and write about them. Try to amplify your thoughts and answers by including the context, the history, the details, and the story of what is coming up in your answers.

Reflecting and Journaling on Your Personality:

1. Are you a perfectionist?
2. Do you expect a great deal from yourself?
3. Are you your own biggest critic?
4. Are you oversensitive to criticism?
5. Do you have a strong need to please people?
6. Who is it hard for you to confront? When is it hard for you to confront people?
7. Is it difficult for you to figure out what you need— and ask for it?
8. Are you a "caretaker"?
9. Do you want people to like you and tend to be overly helpful?
10. Are you overcontrolling?

Again, these are questions to write about and expand on. Include your thoughts about the place of these questions in your history and the details and stories around them. All of these personality traits have the potential to cause us to amass repressed anger in our shadows. Needing to be too good and too controlled and having trouble with confrontations are common and build up emotions in our shadows. Feelings of inferiority that may be revealed by some of these questions also cause us to accumulate reservoirs of rage, despair, and shame.

Reflecting and Journaling on Life Pressures:

1. Do you feel pressure in your job?
2. Do you feel pressure from your partner?
3. Do you feel pressure from your family?
4. Do you feel pressure from your parents?
5. Do you feel pressure from finances?
6. Do you feel pressure from any other big aspects of your life?
7. Do you feel pressure from your age?
8. Make a list of the situations in which you feel angry and cannot express it, whatever the reasons may be.

Once again, amplify and develop your thoughts around each of these questions, the details around the answers, and the stories connected to them. Notice if the patterns are repeating. How do you feel as you are writing about these pressures?

A Final Word

Don't try to do all of this at once. Like training for a marathon, it takes time to develop strength and endurance. The more we journal—the more we explore, develop, and amplify—the more psychologically fit we become for the marathons that are our lives. But it is important that we sit down and think about these things every day and give them a concrete form as well by writing them in our journals. This is the way that ideas and feelings get from our shadows into consciousness. This is how we change how we are living and restructure the patterns in our psyches and in the feelings in our bodies. Set aside time for these activities every day.

Learning the Art and Craft of Loving Ourselves

During my twenties and thirties, if you had asked me if I loved myself, I would not really have understood the question. Deep inside, I had little idea that I only felt loved and respected for my accomplishments and how well I could fulfill the needs and expectations of other people. In my early years of self-reflection, I was shocked to discover how much of myself I had hidden to please others and to create a safe place for myself in the world. The paradox was that, even if I had thought I loved myself at that time, I would have been naïve, because what I believed I loved would have been a fantasy of who I thought I was. This fact is true simply because I didn't know those hidden parts of myself that contained some of my best potentials as well as things I didn't like about myself—repressed fears, desires, and complexes that drove my behavior.

When I first began to look into my heart, my mind, and my history as I approached midlife, I tried to figure out why I had a good life and yet was depressed. Some of the people closest to me accused me of becoming self-absorbed, selfish, and neglectful of my obligations and responsibilities. But I needed to discover the roots of the obligations and responsibilities that I was living by, that were defining who I was, and that seemed to be slowly swallowing my life. And then I had to free how I thought of myself apart from other people's expectations, needs, and desires. This struggle became one of life or death—a struggle I needed to go through before I could understand the meaning of loving myself.

At this point in my journey, I had to be very careful. It is easy to get the wrong idea—the idea that loving myself and having an empowered personality, my little self, would lead me to handle life efficiently and would allow me to move through it with competence and confidence. Actually, the reverse was closer to the truth. Instead of losing my awkwardness, I needed to learn to accept it with grace. Instead of becoming invulnerable, I needed to learn to accept my vulnerability with self-compassion. I needed to learn that I must risk again and again for growth and for love. And I needed to come to understand that my vulnerability would open the door to my authenticity and a greater experience of life.

Empowering my personality did not mean constructing a platform for achieving the good life, triumphant accomplishments, or "enlightened" living. It is the foundation for living a more profound life, in which love and meaning, joy and sorrow, are always two sides of the same coin. It took a depression for me to come to this understanding, and all too often it takes something similar or a tragedy to break the domination and suffocation that exists in our lives and relationships and to open us to the need to love ourselves. In the chapter on "Learning to Love Ourselves" in my book *Sacred Selfishness*, I explain that learning to love ourselves is a process that can only grow as we learn more about ourselves. And loving ourselves is a challenge of the heart to rediscover the feelings and the vitality we were forced to repress in order to form our identities and begin our social development. Our capacity to love in any form depends upon our emotional awareness. Our feelings do more than connect us to life, however. They hold the key to living a life of depth—full of imagination, animation, and an awareness of being close to all life and to loving ourselves.

In my *Sacred Selfishness Workbook*, which is free on my website (www.budharris.com) I offer a path for opening the door to self-love, one step at a time:

1. Remember, love is difficult, the poet Rilke explains, in contrast to the sentimental way we like to think about it. Review your thoughts about love. Do you think it should just bring happiness, ease, or at least security? Do explosions, struggles, and failure make you think love has failed? Life isn't easy, and love can't be easy either.

2. Cultivating self-love is an odyssey with moments of difficulty and joy. It's an excursion into knowing ourselves, of asking whether what we are doing is adding to or diminishing how we feel about ourselves.

3. Self-love challenges the boundaries of how we have fenced ourselves into practicality, conventional wisdom, and other people's perspectives. We must gently ask ourselves whose voice we are really hearing in our head. Is it the voice of our heart? Is it the voice of our Self?

4. Self-love isn't self-indulgent. It isn't shopping sprees, outlandish vacations, sneaking sweets, or pouting moods. It is the commitment to growing in self-knowledge and in our capacity to love. Remembering to take the time for reflection isn't egocentric; it is the key to having the kind of vitality that overflows.

5. Self-love is the foundation that determines how strongly we can give and receive love. Without it, our relationships will crumble under the slightest storm. Take the responsibility for understanding your fears and needs and facing them in a loving way.

6. Self-love rests on self-forgiveness, being able to understand who we were when we failed ourselves, and what needs, hurts, fears, and deprivations were driving us. Only then can we meet ourselves with compassion and kindness. This is why our growth in self-understanding brings healing and reconciliation with our essential selves.

7. Self-love is learning how to be tough with ourselves and taking the driver's seat in our life when we need to break a destructive mood or habit. We must remember that being tough with ourselves means being committed and energetic, having high standards and tenacity. Being tough with ourselves is the opposite of being hard on ourselves, which means being

perfectionistic, self-critical, self-punishing, and un-accepting of our mistakes and weaknesses.

It takes an empowered personality to face the journey, the commitment, the struggles, and the sacrifices we will encounter in the subsequent steps in our individuation process. It also takes an empowered personality to realize the joy and gratitude in this process and to stay grounded and centered, without becoming inflated or caught in il-lusions of power that can cause us to fly too close to the sun and then crash.

As new steps unfold for helping to empower ourselves, one of the first things we confront are our shadows, the parts of ourselves and our deep emotional capacity that most of us have been taught to repress. However, we of-ten avoid confronting our shadows by hiding behind our conventional definitions of ourselves, our responsibilities, our obligations, and the busyness that they impose. This is actually a defense against facing ourselves. Initially, this kind of avoidance was my first line of defense against fac-ing my bigger Self and developing an ongoing, deep in-ner conversation with myself. So then I had to gather the fortitude to stand up and find the true strength hidden in my shadow and stop being swallowed by my own life.

As my journey continued, I had to learn how to meet the poor, the beggars, the prisoners, and the wounded within myself, again and again, in order to enter the places I had previously desired to be immune to. These were the parts of my shadow and my anima (your animus, if you are a woman) that were the gateways to my authenticity and integrity and the foundation for a full life.

Finally, I had to have the strength to encounter the big Self—the greater wisdom center, image of the Divine, and carrier of all the potentials of my life—an experience that Dr. Jung noted was initially a defeat for my little self, my everyday personality. This encounter, too, occurs over and over, once we have realized this point. It is a defeat for our little self, which actually must be strong enough to sacrifice itself to the Self, as it learns to stop seeking power over our lives and learns to seek a different kind of power, the power of love through our experiences of life.

The Groundwork for Becoming Self-Reliant

As we grow up and develop our little self—our personality, an identity that will help us learn the skills and attitudes that will facilitate our taking a place in society—the necessities of this journey, as I have written previously, cause us to become disconnected, disassociated, and to some extent alienated from parts of ourselves. In other words, as we form our identities, we also create our shadows. These dissonances can be large or small, depending upon the environment in which we grew up. They often produce emotions that scare us, but in reality they are calling us to heal these splits.

As I shared in chapter 2, becoming rooted in our own internal reality starts with learning how to be open to our emotions, instead of looking for how to change, repress, and deny them. Our emotions lead the way for us to remain connected with ourselves, in spite of what is going on in our inner and outer worlds. What this means is that our emotional awareness becomes the guide to helping us to reconnect with the "split-off" aspects of ourselves, the wounded parts of ourselves and to nurture our ability to revitalize and transform ourselves. Yet for reconnection and revitalization to maintain their course, it is important to continue to empower our little self, in order to give it the strength and breadth for the development of our whole personality.

The next step in empowering our little self is to understand the four basic archetypal foundation stones that support our personality. We need to heal and develop these support systems before we can go on in our individuation process and forge an authentic life, in connection with our greater Self. These four archetypal foundation stones are the conduits of powerful, instinctual energies. (By instinctual energies, I mean energies that are inherent in our nature.) They are as follows:

1. the Mother Instinct
2. the Father Instinct
3. the Power Instinct
4. the Eros Instinct

These four cornerstones in our personality are frequently either diminished or wounded as we grow up. Empowering our ego means we must heal, recover, and renew these parts of ourselves, and doing this is a vital aspect of our analytic work.

The Mother Instinct is the principal archetypal foundation in our personality, and it reflects the positive side of the Great Mother archetype. This image reflects our need for self-care and the capacity within ourselves to provide that care. In the positive sense, the word *mother* represents someone who is able to bring forth life and is committed to nourishing and supporting it. From the psychological standpoint, we have an inherent need to be able to nourish ourselves; to nurture ourselves; to support and heal ourselves; and to honor, respect, and effectively take care of ourselves. If our Mother Instinct is damaged or undeveloped, we won't know how to nurture and sustain ourselves, and we will end up turning all kinds of destructive negativity toward ourselves that will diminish and block our capacity to live vital lives. Our book *Into the Heart of the Feminine: Facing the Death Mother Archetype to Reclaim Love, Strength, and Vitality* provides a roadmap to healing that part of ourselves and, in essence, to learning how to mother ourselves and our potentials. Though it may be hidden deep inside, we all have the capacity to like, nourish, and take loving care of ourselves.

The Father Instinct is another powerful source of energy and direction within us. In its positive sense as the Great Father archetype, it reflects our need to become self-reliant, autonomous, and independent and to initiate our lives with a spirit of creativity. It nourishes courage and, with the Great Mother archetype, helps us face the ordeals and suffering in being human. When this part of us is wounded, we find ourselves caught in self-criticism, lethargy, and a state of feeling victimized. It is through the Father Instinct that commitment and accomplishments help us to build a strong, stable personality or little self. This instinct helps us envision goals, initiate a journey toward them, and then work to achieve them. It fortifies our resistance against nature's pull to want to be taken care of and to stay safely away from growth and change. If our Father Instinct has been wounded or is unrealized, its negative form can push us toward inflated, unachievable goals and paralyze us with its own form of self-criticism, undermining every shred of our self-respect.

Both our Mother Instinct and our Father Instinct have been wounded in our culture for over a hundred years. Such cultural wounds become internalized as personal wounds that we all have to confront and heal.

The Power Instinct is a part of ourselves that we often think of as negative. But we all have this instinct as an essential part of our personalities. This is the instinct and archetypal pattern that gives us the ability to experience ourselves as having value because we are able to face life successfully and achieve certain goals. This instinct helps us gain a certain measure of control over our lives and their direction. Without the support of the Power Instinct, we find it difficult to form a conscious identity and independence from our dependency needs. It is important for us to learn how to have goals from our mothers and fathers. As soon as our ego has a goal, we need the Power Instinct to become activated and released, to flow into the ego to help it achieve that goal. The more comfortable our ego becomes with this process, the more we gain a sense of confidence and self-respect.

Only experiences of accomplishment can free us from a compulsive need to prove ourselves ceaselessly. A deep feeling of inferiority can force us into a destructive identification with our Power Instinct that will leave us enmeshed in desires for power and control. It is essential for us not to repress our Power Instinct but to healthily nurture it, to "mother" it. It is also just as important to "father" it, to direct its use in a positive way to help us become self-confident and self-reliant. When we learn that we have the ability to do real and meaningful things, we are better able to relax and enjoy life. Then we no longer have to prove ourselves and live in the constant tension of self-criticism and performance anxiety.

The Eros Instinct moves us to want to relate to the world, other people, and ourselves. In the Jungian sense, Eros generally means an interest in personal relatedness and the capacity to work for conciliation and reconciliation. The Eros Instinct evokes self-integration, subjectivity, and the concerns of individuals. In our world of driven activity, it protects us by standing for earthly qualities like stillness, reflection, being, and openness. It is the motivational force behind our emotional attachments that range from sexuality to friendships. It also supports our love of life and our involvements with our hobbies, professions, art, and other fulfilling activities. When our Eros Instinct is wounded, we may become alienated from ourselves and others. Our relationships may be built on power, and we will be compelled to try to maneuver others into being what we think we want or need. Our intimate lives may be characterized as impersonal or based on emotional fusion, and our feeling for life in general will become dried up and depressed. We may feel like we are just "turning the crank" until our time runs out, or we may be saying to ourselves, "If this is it, it's not worth living."

"Know thyself" is a phrase that is as old as western civilization. It often seems selfish in our culture to prioritize our connections to our inner selves and reality, but actually, the reverse is true. Unless we understand what is happening within ourselves and can take responsibility for it and heal the wound to our Eros Instinct, we cannot appreciate other people as themselves. Healthy relationships can only come when we know ourselves and our inner reality, stand grounded in ourselves, and accept others as the people they are.

■ ■ ■

You may remember Elizabeth from earlier in this chapter and before. She realized how serious and powerful her emotions were and chose to go to an analyst for support and direction. As she worked through her rage and sadness with her analyst's help, she began new efforts in her life and started to reactivate her Mother Instinct to nourish and nurture herself. As Elizabeth began to respect her rage and the energy it held for her and to open up in other ways, her analyst asked her some new questions about fear for her to consider:

How is fear affecting your life?
Why are you so afraid of being poor—
in your words, a "bag lady?"
Why are you so afraid of being alone?

As Elizabeth and her analyst worked for several months on these questions, it became apparent to her that working with these questions had two purposes. The first one was to broaden and strengthen her inner Mother Instinct, her ability to nourish herself, trust herself, and trust life. The second aim of these questions was to help activate her Father Instinct, her ability to initiate a new life with courage and creativity.

While they were working on these issues during these several months, Elizabeth journaled all of her thoughts about the questions and how her history had played into them. She watched her dreams carefully, wrote them down in her journal, and then carefully considered all of this material alone and with her analyst. Finally, after feeling they had reached firmer ground, her analyst asked another question:

What would you do if you were not afraid?

Answering that question took Elizabeth to graduate school and to her new vocation of becoming a pastoral counselor. In a few more years, she asked herself this question once again and that answer carried her on to Zurich to grow, study, and enlarge herself even more. By learning to value herself and her capacities and accomplishments, she activated the Power Instinct within herself to do new, real, and meaningful things in her life. And as her Eros Instinct increased, she was no longer alienated from some of her strongest qualities, and she became like a magnet, attracting new relationships and friendships.

You may also remember David, whom I mentioned in chapter 3. David is a retired physics professor living in an upscale retirement home. He was living a comfortable life in an emotional and spiritual atmosphere of lethargy. He was seeing me because his wife was tired of his depression. He told me that he didn't believe in an afterlife. He went on to explain that after we died that was it— there is just the void. So, he concluded, why should he do anything other than seek comfort?

Of course, David isn't the first person I have heard this line of thinking from. Interestingly enough, in my experience, this point of view has come from men who are reasonably affluent and consider themselves somewhat intellectual. In most cases, this point of view and the lethargy that is associated with it infuriate their wives, who then fail to "leave them alone" and "accept them for who they are." I believe a true partner instinctively knows when there is a serious wound to the Mother or Father Instinct in his or her mate. Though he or she may not be able to verbalize it in these terms, when his or her mate doesn't trust life, isn't able to confront his or her moods, and isn't able to initiate a new spirit of being alive within him- or herself, that partner eventually becomes angry, frustrated, and even disgusted.

After David and I had gotten to know each other pretty well, I found out that he had written a number of scientific journal articles. I suggested to David that he write an article from a "feeling" standpoint for a blog or psychological journal. He had the credentials for his article to be considered by many different kinds of journals. I suggested the following topics:

1. How does lethargy affect the life and relationships of a man your age?
2. How does simply wanting comfort and acceptance affect the life and relationships of a man your age?
3. How does such an outlook on the future affect the life and relationships of a man your age?

I explained that the process of developing these writings should help open him up. He was to write to amplify and clarify his thoughts and then develop his idea and fears around each theme. Then he was to honor them and share them with me.

A partner cannot give a mate enough support to heal a wound to his or her Mother or Father Instinct. We each must make that journey for ourselves, and it is never too late for us to heal and grow into a new life. In this case, I was inviting David to confront not only his lethargy, but also the fear he was rationalizing by saying life had no value. In this invitation, I was supporting his Power Instinct to find new value in himself and to face his attitude toward life. I was also inspiring him to strengthen his Eros Instinct by encouraging him to confront his self-alienation.

As I have explained, we call individuation a journey into wholeness because it means the continuous, conscious development of knowing oneself and the growing awareness of our need to know the greater Self. So individuation really begins when we can recognize our wounds in these four fundamental parts of ourselves and seek out the help we need to heal them.

Our instinctual urge toward wholeness and unity within ourselves calls for us to turn inward and forge authentic, compassionate, and responsible ways to reconnect to these four archetypal conduits of our life energy. Healing and wholeness begin here and give us the foundation for developing a vital connection with our greater

Self and the divine energy and destiny that is held within us.

■ ■ ■

It may occur to you that all of these things should have been taken care of as we grew up. But in truth, they aren't. At every transitional level we reach on the spiral staircase of our development, we have to go back down and rework many of them. That was certainly true for me at midlife, and when I entered my fourth quarter, and after my cancer. Did this take a lot of effort? You bet. Was it worth it? I can only say that I have had my share of traumas, sorrow, challenges, and losses, but the inner work has carried me through these events and into a life of vitality beyond what I could have ever imagined.

6

Reflections on the Journey: Singed, Scorched, and Seasoned

Growing up surprised me by turning out to be a life-long endeavor. Initially, I charged into adulthood with so much determination that I didn't think very much about how desperately I was trying to figure out how to be happy and successful. My generation married young, and I got married while still in college. As I've talked with men's groups over the years I have realized that marriage was our attempt at initiation, to force ourselves into the quest for adulthood. Likewise, for many of us, joining the corporate world was an effort to find our place in the culture of grown-ups.

Later, when I stepped out of the corporate world and into my own business, I was trying to step toward a more personal sense of identity. Before taking this step, I spent more than two years planning my new venture and consulting with friends about making this change. During these discussions, I became aware of the underlying layer of dissatisfaction in so many of the men and women I was close to. In addition, I was mentally working out the details and imagining the success that was fueling my courage to take this leap. Such thoroughness backed by the power of dreams, determination, friends, and colleagues led to the success of my business, but not to my fantasized satisfaction. My full engagement paid off, except for the fact I ended up depressed instead of happy.

Even if we need to heal our childhoods, and who doesn't, it must then lead to a full engagement in life for individuation to proceed. Living passionately, according to Jung, will bring us to the right path even if we're doing the wrong thing to begin with. Living passionately also brings a certain singeing. Singeing comes from being near to or in the flame, the flame of being involved wholeheartedly in life and facing its failures, problems, blocks, and wounds head on. It also means reflecting upon such experiences and searching for meaning in them. Trying to "get it right" in advance leads to being stuck and constantly spinning our wheels. A full engagement generates the material for us to reflect on that builds our self-awareness and opens the doors to new life.

My wife, Massimilla, and I have often talked about how accepting the failure of our dreams, ideals, and what we thought we knew about life has dropped us into the singeing flames of transformation. This acceptance isn't easy, and we've had to learn to honor our grief and bitterness as part of the transformative work. Acceptance is a turning point. It means we face the fire of our own experiences and quit trying to avoid the necessary psychological death of an old self that precedes breaking through our limitations and being reborn. Too often we defend against our pain and the transformative process by turning our symptoms into enemies that we want to banish, suppress, or defeat. Transformation means giving up our defense structure of creating a war within ourselves—the structure that wants to prevent us from seeking out the truth of our own reality. This approach is the road less traveled; it is countercultural, and it negates our ideas of control, rationality, and fixing problems. But it allowed me to turn my depression into a path of deep healing and reflection and the source of a new life.

With reflection, the scorching began. I realized I was not who I thought I was. I was not a unique individual living a creative life, as most of my business friends imagined, who would have answered immediately, "Of course," if you had asked him if he loved himself. It scorches the soul to realize you are living a pattern designed collectively by family, society, church, job, and traditions. The only thing unique about it was how my childhood wounds and successes operated to shape the living of this pattern. I was depressed and collapsing and faced with the question, "Can you accept this person and love him?" Scorching meant accepting that my most treasured activities—planning, dreaming, and pursuing the dream—were narcotizing my fear.

This acceptance is difficult, and I see the need for it almost daily as I work and teach. I wish I knew how to make it easier for people, but it is the necessary cleansing fire. All too often our most successful actions are in the service of flight. I was admired for being ambitious, courageous, taking risks, and being hard working and smart enough to pursue my dreams. And love was involved, for I loved my family and wanted a better life for them. Plus, I firmly believed I was fulfilling my obligations. Make no mistake about this fact either: I'm glad I did it! I'm glad because the experience gave me a foundation of courage to take risks that is still alive today. I'm glad because this experience taught me that the journey into hell is the first step in discovering the deep well of psychic energy within, which ultimately makes love and joy equal parts of life. And I'm glad that I have become a seasoned guide in this process, like the ones I was so fortunate to have had.

The reality is that our culture teaches us to run harder and achieve more in order to avoid confronting ourselves, the earlier struggles and realities in our past, and the fiction we are creating and thinking of as our lives. Depression and chaos were the big Self's way of stopping me, calling for healing, and trying to force self-confrontation. But I still had a choice. I could have chosen to seek a conventional cure and some semblance of normal functioning. Or I could have repressed my inner conflicts so vigorously that I could have forced them into becoming an illness. Actually, I believed at the time I would have a heart attack before I was forty if I stayed on the same path. Something inside warned me of this danger, and thankfully, I listened and made the second choice of journeying into the unknown land of seeking to know myself.

To be familiar with myth is to know that Odysseus, Aeneas, Faust, and others had to go into the underworld to find vital wisdom. Dante wrote his great poem to show the rest of us the way. We can only reach heaven through hell, by carrying our cross into the darkness of our fear, shadow, wounds, and failed dreams. Dante started his journey on Good Friday. Anger, sorrow, disappointment, bewilderment, and being singed and scorched are preludes to individuation, to becoming whole, and to realizing the true depth of love and the richness of life available to us. This path is the one that transforms our ego—our little self—and initiates it into a relationship with the Self, the Divine spark within. The archetypal pattern of transformation confronts our small self, and by doing so belies our cultural ideals and self-help books, because we cannot be reborn without dying, and individuation is about being reborn again, and again, and again.

■ ■ ■

How have I become—and how am I becoming—seasoned? To begin with, I've discovered that just like growing up is a lifelong process, so is becoming seasoned. Seasoning is becoming tempered, ripened, salted, modest, and realizing that life is sacred, and if everything is created by the Divine, it is all for me to love. To love a whole, however, doesn't mean I have to love every part. Life and the world are here for me to love, but that doesn't mean that I have to love tragedy or evil. To be seasoned means knowing how to accept and reflect on life and in particular how to be fully engaged in life and reflect on what we are experiencing. Reflection is the process that fosters my growth and makes me stronger at my broken places. This is tempering, and it leaves us like the old soldier who knows how to handle himself in battle or the wise old country woman who knows the cycles of the moon, planting, harvesting, birthing, and dying.

Fear! To be seasoned by fear is to know and accept deep in my heart and stomach that life cannot be fully controlled. It is to know that I and all that I love exist by a slender thread, which may snap at almost any time. It is also to know that the more I try to defend myself past a certain point and stake my sense of safety on controlling life, the more likely I am to set myself up for disappointment and tragedy. Fear has driven me at times to withdraw from life and to close in on myself, and thereby, I risked the biggest tragedy of all—never being fully alive and engaged. I have also found that fear can be sneaky. It can cause me to have an illusion of being fully engaged while, at the same time, I am secretly avoiding the risks of transformation, dying to an old life, and being born into a new one whose future is uncertain and at best only a dream.

When I think of being seasoned, I remember Hemingway's lines in *A Farewell to Arms* that I quoted earlier: "If people bring so much courage to this world the world has to kill them to break them, so of course it kills them. The world breaks everyone and afterward many are strong at the broken places. But those that will not break, it kills. It kills the very good and the very gentle and the very brave impartially. If you are none of these you can be sure it will kill you too, but there will be no special hurry."

It saddens me to know that to live, and to live passionately, we must be willing to be broken. But if we are willing to be broken and still have the courage to reflect on these events, we are transformed. The creative spirit of the Divine that I experience through the big Self shapes life as a journey of personal transformation. Being singed and scorched can lead to awakening. When I follow the path of individuation, the inner journey, awakening, leads to a disciplined process of seeking self-knowledge that will strengthen and fortify me. Then I gain the fortitude to accept, and I must constantly remind myself of this, that it is through conflict, tension, and suffering that I, we, and the world are differentiated and grow. True peace comes when I can accept this dynamism.

Writing has been a good example of a journey of struggle that singed, scorched, and seasoned me. Writing morphed into a torture, a torture of risking myself, seeking acceptance, and being rejected in ways so painful they brought up the feelings of every stinging childhood rejection. I became afraid of facing the red pen of an editor, the rejection letters of publishers, and the criticism of readers. While these were strong fears, there were deeper ones: the fear of not being heard, of not being able to speak to things that other people are afraid of, too. Even as I write this, an image comes to mind, and I find myself wanting to pick up that serious-faced eight-year-old boy that I once was. I want to hold him tight and say, "Speak to me. I will listen. Tell me what you are afraid of, what makes you happy." Here is the root of my fear, and I want to comfort it.

I have followed Dr. Jung's advice that if you do the wrong thing with all your heart, you will end up at the right place. I've pursued writing with all of my heart for more than twenty years, and it has become the right place. I began writing with a quotation from Ibsen on my desk. It reads, "To live is to war with trolls in heart and soul. To write is to sit in judgment on oneself."

Writing shaped and formed me as it led me to mountaintops of hope and dashed me at other times into despair. Every book is a personal journey in which there is no escaping my history, my shadow, and my complexes. When every manuscript is finished, the same questions remain: "Was it all too painful?" "Can I learn to write again?" "Can I learn to dream again?" So far, the answer has always been yes.

Becoming seasoned is also a process like peeling an onion, as I am forced to differentiate myself from the values, ideals, wisdom, and other things that I have built my life and identity upon. Of course, my shadow and anima goad me along this path mercilessly. Some years ago, I awakened with a start from a dream in which a woman was charging at me with a knife, clearly intending to stab me repeatedly. Alarmed and curious, I approached her carefully in active imagination and asked her why she was attacking me. She answered, "I want to cut you badly so you will feel my pain. I want you to feel the pain I suffer, because you don't have the guts to hate the people who have hurt you."

In this interaction, I am learning about the other within me who knows it is OK and often healthy to hate those who hurt, threatened, and diminished me when I was small or when I couldn't defend myself and caused fear, anxiety, or shame to be structured into my personality. Coming home to myself means finding the other within, the other who shows up in dreams and fantasies as a stranger. But who is the one who sees the other side of our internalized values, like hate is bad or forgiveness is good or that we need to let go of past hurts and anger?

This fiery woman was one of the many inner strangers I've met on this journey. Some of them approach me aggressively, others casually or by stealth because I have repressed them so strongly. To consider openly hating someone caused my self-image to be broken once again. These meetings and my reflections on them caused my self-image to be broken repeatedly until I became seasoned enough to realize that deep feelings from any time in my life—whether positive or negative—need to be fully experienced and processed through my reflections. As this process seasoned me, I discovered that forgiveness (when it wasn't sought) and letting go are no longer relevant. I have found the truth in the assertion of author and Jungian analyst June Singer that we need to come to the place of fully accepting our deepest emotions and be able to hate without the need for retribution and love without possessiveness. Every inner stranger I accept releases an amazing amount of psychic energy, and I feel more whole, more fully human.

Grief, illness, and death also have important places in seasoning. I share some of my thoughts on grief and death in my upcoming book, *Radical Hope and the Healing Power of Illness: A Jungian Guide to Exploring the Body, Mind, Spirit Connection to Healing*. In conclusion, I think the four truths that I've learned on my journey, the ones included in *The Fire and the Rose*, sum up my thoughts on abundance and limitations.

Four truths have become apparent to me in my own pursuit of self-knowledge as a way of life. First, I have learned that the fundamental assertion in most mystical traditions—that self-knowledge is the way to come to know the Divine—is absolutely true. Self-knowledge releases us from the prison of our personal history, deconditions us from the attitudes of our parents and society, and forces us to work through our losses, hurts, and grief. This act of purification, as the mystics called it, opens us to our depths, to the big Self, the Divine energy within us.

The second truth I realized is that compassion must begin with myself. The cultivation of compassion toward my failures, shortcomings, and humanness opens the door to self-love and makes me a truly compassionate person with others. This process grounds us in our full humanity and supports the self-love implied in the commandment "Love your neighbor as yourself." Self-love anchored in self-knowledge is the underpinning of how well we can give and receive love. Without self-love our structure of relationships will crumble under the pressure of the smallest storms, and our so-called unselfish acts will create an inner cauldron of resentment. I know this from the results of many years when I thought I could be hard on myself and loving to others. The only person I fooled was myself.

Self-love is like water flowing into a pond. When the pond is full, the water will overflow and begin to venture into the world. If we fail to know ourselves, we risk causing our souls to become arid and our hearts to stagnate in fear and defensiveness. What a wonderful paradox—loving ourselves is actually taking care of others.

The third thing I discovered is that a life based on the pursuit of self-knowledge continually takes us back into the world and among our communities. We cannot live a wholehearted life alone. We must participate in all the various relationships, attractions, love, friendships, conflicts, and projections to gain stimulation as well as the content that informs much of our search for self-knowledge.

The fourth and final thing that I gradually became aware of is that something inside me cares about me and my life. If I listen, it speaks to me through my dreams, fantasies, inspiration, and thoughts. When I reflect, journal, and work with my active imagination, it helps to heal my wounds, turn my symptoms and failures into lessons, and aid me in discerning what my soul wants for my life. It does not save me from any of life's difficulties or catastrophes. But when I am suffering, it is there with me.

I have called this something the big Self over the course of my writing. As an analyst, I have studied and worked with the concept of the Self for many years. I've seen the validity of this concept by noting how it works in my life and in the lives of people I counsel professionally. Today, I experience the Self very personally instead of viewing it from the distance of psychological theory. While I am not a theologian, I believe that my interactions with the Self are a true experience of feeling the love of the Divine.

7

The Spiritual Challenges of Aging

Dr. Carl Jung, Dr. Viktor Frankl, and many of our other great doctors of the soul repeatedly point out that it is in our very nature as human beings to seek meaning. In the opening quotation of this book, I chose Dr. Jung's words that "Man cannot stand a meaningless life." After losing all of the people dear to him and personally surviving the concentration camps during World War II, Dr. Frankl concluded that two things are necessary for us to survive, live, and flourish. The first one is to be oriented toward the future, and the second one is to be directed toward a meaning to be fulfilled by our lives in the future. Today, we seem to be living in an era that has left us with more choices than we can comprehend and yet with less meaning that we can find purpose and fulfillment in.

Midlife has become the traditional time when we find ourselves in an emotional wasteland that is calling us to confront ourselves and our lives in order to better understand ourselves and the structures and values that are supporting and driving our lives. This reevaluation requires an inner journey that will help us understand the emotional foundation and the structures of who we are. From this foundation, our lives can begin transforming and evolving into new levels of purpose, meaning, and fulfillment.

This turning point requires a lot of introspection and inner work, and in our productivity-pressured, utilitarian-oriented society, more people are missing this "turn" than are making it. This misfortune leaves us with a host of emotional and physical problems. The reality is that whether we like it or not, it was our experiences of pain, hurt, and anger, which we so often had to repress out of our need for self-preservation, that shaped our personality, our lives, and their course. At midlife, our personality needs to be reexamined and restructured in order to give us a growing and fulfilling future.

Now we are facing another aspect of reality individually and as a culture. We are living thirty years longer than people a few generations ago did. As a result of this new development, our historical views on aging have little to offer us, because they are based on a past we are not repeating. My professional experience over the last twenty years has shown me that, as we approach the fourth quarter in our lives, we actually face another "wasteland" experience, in which we are being instinctively called again, in an even deeper way, to see ourselves as whole and to create out of our now richer experience a new vision of who we are and the myth we are living by. And by the myth, I mean the structure of values that give us meaning, vitality, and a sense of direction and purpose for our lives. This is a time we are invited to go deep inside ourselves and develop a new myth that will carry us through the rest of our lives. Developing this new myth is the spiritual challenge for this time in our lives.

This is another great turning point that is calling us to come home to ourselves, our authentic selves. This is the transformational period I have been discussing in this book when, once again, it pays for us to go deeper into our inner quest for healing, wholeness, and authentic self so that we can free our most profound potentials to be engaged in life. Over the years, I've learned that after completing a period of transformation, we find ourselves feeling stronger, enriched, enlarged, and more at home, within ourselves and the world, than we did before. When we follow the pattern of our nature, transformation unlocks additional aspects of our future that we could never have imagined and keeps us from being ensnared by our past. Armed with this information, we can easily keep in mind that the true norm is change, for we are continually in process.

During my midlife transformation period, which I share in my memoir *Cracking Open*, I had a vision of Buddy, my eight-year-old self, sitting across the table from me as I was having a cup of coffee in a Shoney's Big Boy restaurant in my old hometown. Later, he reappeared in a dream and asked me, "What have you done with my life?" This image stays with me constantly and reminds me that I am in the fourth quarter of my life. If you read that section of my memoir, you will see my father's history and some of my own that allowed football to be a metaphor for the game of life. When he was a coach in his younger years, one of my father's favorite sayings was, "You want to play your strongest game in the fourth quarter."

When I look into the image of Buddy's eyes and hear the words "What have you done with my life?" I remember that I am in the fourth quarter and that I want to be fully in the game, and by the end of the game, I want to have left everything I had on the playing field.

Reflections on Dying

Early one morning, when I was in my early fifties, I woke up weeping and could not stop. When my wife, Massimilla, awakened, she was shocked to find me quietly weeping in our living room. As we talked, I realized that I was weeping for my own death.

When we begin to talk about death seriously, the first thing that comes up is our fear of death. Our fear leads to denial and an inability to form a perspective on what death can mean to our lives. Fear and denial rigidify the defensive stance of our egos—our little selves—and diminishes or inhibits their ability to face the transformative cycles through which we grow, the life-death-rebirth processes that are a necessary part of our individuation process. When denied and repressed, our fear of death lurks in the depths of our psyche like a great white shark, and its presence is ultimately reflected in our fear of becoming fully alive. This primitive devouring presence of danger can become reflected in the fears we harbor about our own necessary transformations and a future defined by the Self, rather than our values, goals, and desires.

One of the main questions, then, becomes, how does individuation, the dream of a life that fulfills its unique potentials, both help us and require us to forge a perspective on death and the afterlife? Our religious heritages are closely connected to death, and they tell us in their own ways that death should inform life and how we live in this life will affect how we live in the afterlife. That these ideas are reflected throughout history and, in some form, in almost every religion makes them archetypal. That is why Jung thought it was critical to our wholeness to consider them. Jung knew that our ideas about death and the afterlife can either inform or cripple how we live, can limit us to the bounds of our intellects or open us to the inspiring and healing powers of our emotions and the expanses of our mythopoetic capacities. We have an inherent longing to come up with our own conclusions about these mysteries. Our same religious history,

Jung thought, reflects an additional longing that is often buried so deep that we may not even be aware of it. This longing is to have our lives connected to something greater than ourselves, something infinite, so we can embody something essential to ensure that our life matters.

Massimilla and I find that our individuation process, the guiding focus of our lives, challenges us to begin facing death in two special ways. The first one is when we fully realize that we grow psychologically and spiritually by the process of transformation—the cycle of life, death, and rebirth—that is facilitated by our emotional healing and growing consciousness. As we are continuing to transform, we are facing another symbolic death, an encounter with the big Self, the transcendent, the Divine within us. This encounter, which necessitates a death and a rebirth of our ego, our little self, also leads us toward thoughts of the beyond.

Jungian psychology is frequently so challenging to understand that we often have to remind ourselves that individuation is not an intellectual activity. It is based upon our ability to engage in life actively, reflect on our experiences, listen to our unconscious, and develop the emotional capacities that enable us to fully engage in life. The events in the individuation process are there to push us beyond the ways our histories, families, and culture have defined us. In this process, we must be willing to face ourselves, confront the many faces in our shadows, transform their emotional power over us, and thereby transform our lives. Here, again, is the transformative cycle, the symbolic life-death-rebirth process. As we live this process, we must continually help old parts of us die and be willing to live in the betwixt and between state of not knowing who we fully are, until the new parts of our personality have emerged. In this way, if we fully pursue individuation, we will consciously and intentionally encounter death as part of an archetypal format of growth that is an integral part of life.

Massimilla and I have found that realizing the greater Self is a powerful experience of "living through death," which significantly changes our attitudes toward life, eternity, and the beyond. As we have come to know the presence of the Self and learned to relate to it and accept it as the guiding spirit in our lives, this entire process has brought comfort to the way we feel about approaching death. In religious terms, it is like saying, "God is with us."

In other words, we must go forward by "dying into life," facing the deaths needed in our individuation in order to fulfill and live the broader potentials within us, to open our capacities to love more completely, and to be sure that when death finds us, we are fully alive. Individuation means accepting the reality of our unconscious, sacrificing our ego control of our lives, and with discernment, listening to the superior intelligence of the Self to guide us through life. We wonder, in the long run, how often we are like the people we meet, who are more afraid of facing themselves; of questioning their values, ideas, and complexes; and of dying into life than they are of literally dying. As part of the journey, it is helpful if we can take this line of questioning a step further and ask ourselves if our fear of dying into life is really our fear of living fully.

Dying into life though individuation and knowing that the greater Self is supporting us has lessened our fear of death, perhaps even eliminated it. At the same time, it has greatly lessened our fear of life. Most of us don't even know we have a fear of life, or how great that fear is, until individuation leads us into the full acceptance of life's horror and beauty, its wholeness and our wholeness, our true strengths and our real weaknesses, our ability to love, our capacity for rage, our experience of ecstasy, and our despair. Dying into life continually increases our ability to stop living in denial, and to see how integral a part of our lives death truly is, and how thoroughly it is woven into the fabric of our existence. Death and the afterlife are still mysteries, but we can be very much in touch with them and informed by them.

Old Masters: After Eighty Some People Don't Retire, They Reign
—*New York Times*, October 26, 2014

In this lovely and inspiring article, Lewis H. Lapham, an old master himself and former editor of *Harper's Magazine* and *Lapham's Quarterly*, shared the portraits of eleven men and women in their eighties and nineties who are successful in their fields, refuse to rest on their laurels, and continue unceasing to discover or create something new.

In it he listed Frederick Wiseman, an eighty-four-year-old filmmaker; T. Boone Pickens, chairman of B. P. Capital Management, age eighty-six; Justice Ruth Bader Ginsburg, eighty-one, who remarked, "There's a sense that time is precious and you should enjoy and thrive in what you are doing to the hilt"; Roy Haynes, eighty-nine, jazz drummer and bandleader; Edward O. Wilson, eighty-five, naturalist and writer; Ginette Bedland, eighty-one, long distance runner; and Ellsworth Kelly, ninety-one, an artist who said, "It's one thing about getting older. You see more...Every day I'm continuing to see things. That's why there are more paintings."

Then there is Carmen Herrera, ninety-nine. Carmen sold her first painting at eighty-nine. Now she has paintings displayed at the Museum of Modern Art and the Tate Museum. Tony Bennett, age eighty-eight, is still singing and performing; Christopher Plummer is still acting at eighty-four; and R. O. Blechman, eighty-four, illustrator and author, said in his book *Dear James: Letters to a Young Illustrator*, "I think I'm freer now. I think I'm better. It's crazy. As it goes downhill, I'm going up."

Lewis Lapham notes in the article, "I begin to understand that failure is its own reward. It is in the effort to close the distance between the work imagined and the work achieved wherein it is to be found that the ceaseless labor is the freedom of play, that what's at stake isn't a reflection in the mirror of fame but the escape from the prison of the self." Escape from the prison of the little self and serving life beyond this is one of the main things I'm devoting this book to. Lewis ends the article by saying, "And the lesson I'm now almost old enough to learn: that the tree of knowledge and the fountain of youth are one and the same." We need to examine the experiences of people who live with passion and purpose. What traits set them apart? Like Lewis Lapham, they have done the work to know what matters to them and are committed to living forward with purpose and creativity.

The very idea of reigning as an old master is incredibly inspiring to me. Just think—to become an old master in your own life and to let the journey unfold your creativity and your vocation and keep your love of life engaged.

In the same *New York Times Magazine*, there was an article on aging as a state of mind, which stated that surrounding ourselves with music and an environment and décor from our younger years can help keep our attitudes young. I think that this shows that the spirit of how we live is also a very important factor in our lives. The old masters stayed in the arena and ambience of their creative pursuits. It also makes me wonder if staying in mixed-age communities as long as possible isn't helpful. I want to keep what all too often is thought of as a youthful state of mind that looks to the future, is ambitious, desires love, and yet at the same time is grounded in the present and gratitude—and wants to serve a meaningful purpose, rather than being held back by fear.

In my sixties, I had a dream that I was starring in a modern version of William Shakespeare's play *King Lear*. I was walking up and down the aisles of a department store in full costume. I didn't know the lines and had lost my script, which was written in large letters that I could easily read. I wanted to speak loudly, but the cue cards weren't helpful, and I was saying the wrong words. As I reflected on the dream, I remembered that I had spent the first ten years of my adult life in department stores as a buyer and senior executive. The atmosphere in that business was tense, exciting at times, and very competitive. All of the senior executives I knew in those years felt a lot of anxiety. In fact, we lived and worked in a general atmosphere of anxiety. The dream reminded me of how easily I can step back into that old mental state of feeling tense and anxious, since I was in the dreamscape of a department store. At the same time, I see King Lear as a figure who wanted to "retire" in pleasure, wealth, and comfort, He wanted to give up his responsibility to govern the country, a God-given right and duty in his day. By giving up his kingship, he created tragedy in his family and betrayal and more tragedy in his court. With no new king, the kingdom became fragmented and torn with inner wars as well.

This dream presents a scary, psychological picture of what was going on in my psyche and the dark potential approach my life would take, if I didn't change. In my writing and creative work, I had slipped back into the department store mentality and was trying to drive my creativity with fear and anxiety. During my reflection about the dream, I realized that I needed to change. I needed to take a position of leadership and control in my creative life and govern myself in a way that honored the creative flame that wanted to leap up, while at the same time anchoring myself more firmly in my psychological depths. Pressure can wear us out. It exhausted Lear, who wanted to simply get out, rather than taking up his responsibility to rule and transform the situation.

Tragedy, in the classical Greek sense, results from a lack of self-awareness and consciousness. The dream was telling me to wake up and become more conscious. The dream became very important to me, and as I was contemplating its story and its images, I immediately became more relaxed, slept better, and finished two books that I had been working on. There is a huge difference between having a ruling principle in my personality like King Lear and one like one of the old masters Lewis Lapham wrote about.

Changing and Re-creating Ourselves Changes and Re-creates the World

As I was writing this manuscript, I took a break to watch *A Matter of Heart*, which is a movie about Dr. Jung that is filled with conversations with people who knew him well. In the movie, Dr. Jung is quoted as writing,

> The great events of world history are, at bottom,
> profoundly unimportant. In the last analysis,
> the essential thing is the life of the individual.

> This alone makes history, here alone do the
> great transformations first take place, and
> the whole future, the whole history of the
> world ultimately springs as a giant summation
> from these hidden sources in individuals.

> In our most private and most subjective
> lives, we are not only the passive witnesses

of our age, and its sufferers, but also its makers. We make our own epoch.

This quotation reminds me that every one of us is important. Each one of us can help change history and move the benefits of life forward, if we face this new challenge of longer life head on, transforming and deepening ourselves and letting the results of these transformations flow into the world. Dr. Jung's quotation brings to mind for me another one of my favorite stories, "The Star Thrower," from a book by the well-known twentieth-century anthropologist Loren Eisley, who wrote compassionate, probing meditations on the natural world. The theme of this story, which is written far more beautifully than I can relate it here, revolves around a man living on a distant island in the Pacific that has long open beaches, even though it is also a resort. As the tide goes out, long-limbed starfish lay stranded on the sand, dying slowly without the seawater.

The man is walking along the beach, checking to see which starfish are still alive. He reaches down, picks up the living creature, and flings it into the sea. When asked if he was a collector, he replies with a definite "No!" His actions speak for him, as he saves the ones that he can by throwing them back into the sea. In addition to him, there are many collectors of starfish on the beach, picking them up to keep and to sell. The man seems to be attempting an impossible job, because there are so many starfish, and he can only save a few of them, but he seems to know it makes a huge difference to each one that is saved and given new life. The star thrower is one who loves life. We may feel like star throwers at times, working against the tide, but we must love life like the star thrower did, and live it that way, knowing, as Dr. Jung said, that it makes a difference how we choose to live our lives.

I had read another article in the *New York Times* business section before I read the article "Old Masters Reign." This article was about four CEOs of sizeable companies who were in their midnineties. They were bringing a beneficial atmosphere to their companies and were living with balance and vigor. Of course, there are many people who pursue success with far more negative values. But these four people were star throwers—inspiring.

We don't have to move mountains or revolutionize the world. We just need for enough of us to face the future, transform ourselves, and become life givers in the ambience of our own surroundings. To become a life giver is a spiritual challenge.

Transforming ourselves in the fourth quarter of life brings us the greatest freedom in our lives. It is the kind of freedom to be at home in ourselves, in our lives, and to know we are making a contribution to life. Of course, transforming ourselves and gaining this kind of freedom involves careful attention, awareness, and discipline. It also means that we will be serving something greater than ourselves that gives purpose and joy to our lives. It means we will naturally care about other people in little ways, every day, by being who we are. The alternative is to live a shrinking life at the default setting, the fear-driven smallness of our society, along with the devouring sense of having had something valuable and having lost it. It is the difference between being a life giver and a collector.

Conclusion

I began this book by letting you know of my surprise at being almost eighty years old and working and creating at a level I had never dreamed I would at this age! In this book, I have also shared with you my own experience of this vitality, as well as similar stories of other people that show the immense opportunities we have in the fourth quarter of our lives today.

Our reality is that we are living up to thirty years longer than people just a few years ahead of us did. This fact means that we have no societal history to help us understand how to prepare for and live into this time in our lives. We have no guidelines for our transition into this period in our lives.

In addition, we are still overdependent on the ideas that willpower, technology, and science can help us to live happy, fulfilling lives. If we walk blindly into and through this period of our lives without facing the true reality of it, what it means for us and what its potentials are—if we don't define it for *ourselves*—then someone else and some other force will define it for us. And by doing so, they will define *us*.

Facing a transition point, such as entering the fourth quarter of life, means the loss of much of what has typically defined us as individuals in the past. In the face of this loss, we may try to hang on to the vestiges of our old selves and our old dreams until we become hollow versions of them. We can also simply try to slide comfortably into the roles that our family, society, and the media have described for us. Or, as I have shared in this book, we can dedicate ourselves to the discovery of a new self, a personhood of true independence who, in his or her process of development and living, contributes to life in its largest sense.

That is the challenge of this book and the journey it is inviting you to begin...

By aging strong, we will be living forward. By living forward, we will inherently be tapping into our capacity to give back—creating a better world for our families, for our communities, for all.

■　■　■

As we heal and transform ourselves, as we live strongly into the future, we will be helping to lift the burdens of our familial and cultural histories from the younger generations. We will also be creating a new vision of the future for our culture, as we transition and grow into a whole new life beyond what we have imagined for ourselves.

We can be creative, accomplish new things, find new vocations and new callings, learn to thrive, have a sense of wonder, and have a new sense of security in life, as well as deeper emotional connections, wisdom, and a newfound joy in living. As we slow down physically, we can grow psychologically and spiritually.

The most exciting part of this story is that the more we pursue this larger life by deepening and transforming ourselves in this fourth quarter of our lives, the bigger our gift to our families, friends, community, and culture becomes. Let us meet this challenge and turn it into one of the greatest opportunities in our human history by originating a new way forward. Let us shape our lives from the inside out and be fully alive with grace and passion by living our lives forward to their fullest extent while, at the same time, giving back to our communities and to our world.

A Note of Thanks

Whether you received *Aging Strong: The Extraordinary Gift of a Longer Life* as a gift, borrowed it from a friend, or purchased it yourself, we're glad you read it. We think that Bud Harris is a refreshing, challenging, and inspiring voice and we hope you will share this book and his thoughts with your family and friends. If you would like to learn more about Bud Harris, Ph.D. and his work, please visit: www.budharris.com or https://www.facebook.com/BudHarrisPh.D.

About the Author

B ud Harris, Ph.D, as a Jungian analyst, writer and lecturer, has dedicated his life to helping people grow through their challenges and life situations into becoming "the best versions of themselves." Bud originally became a businessman in the corporate world and then owned his own business. Though very successful, he began to search for a new version of himself and life when, at age thirty-five, he became dissatisfied with his accomplishments in business and was challenged by serious illness in his family. At this point, Bud returned to graduate school to become a psychotherapist. After earning his Ph.D. in psychology and practicing as a psychotherapist and psychologist, he experienced the call to further his growth and become a Jungian analyst. He then moved to Zurich, Switzerland, where he trained for over five years and graduated from the C. G. Jung Institute. Bud is the author of thirteen informing and inspiring books. He writes and teaches with his wife, Jungian analyst, Massimilla Harris, Ph.D., and lectures widely. Bud and Massimilla both practice as Jungian analysts in Asheville, North Carolina. For more information about his practice and work, visit: www.budharris.com or https://www.facebook.com/BudHarrisPh.D.